M000039800

every teen girl's little pink book of prayers

by Cathy Bartel

Harrison House
Tulsa, Oklahoma

13 11 12 10 09   10 9 8 7 6 5 4 3 2 1

dedication

I dedicate this *little pink book* to my sweet nieces: Ashley, Britt', Savannah, and little Taylor. The Lord bless you and keep you and make His face shine upon you and enlighten you and be gracious to you; The Lord lift up His countenance upon you and give you peace (Num. 6:24-26). May He give you the desire of your heart and make all your plans succeed.

I pray that you know how loved and cherished you are by Jesus and your family. Each of you is a gift and you bring so much joy to all who know you. I love you and I'm so thankful I get to be your auntie.

Love always,
Auntie Cath' xox

acknowledgment

Thank You, Father, for all of the wonderful girls at Northstar—from the little ones on up. What a privilege it is to serve side by side and come together to worship You. Thank You for women and girls who continually encourage one another and demonstrate Your love in their homes, schools, neighborhoods, and workplaces. You have brought us all together to shine You, Lord. Thank You also for all of these gals who know You as the God Who answers prayer and also know You and Your voice.

Grace and peace be multiplied to all of these beautiful ladies!

To Julie, Becky, Jenn, Lindsay, Chris, Johnie & Jenn, Katie, Elaine (Mum), and Blaine THANK YOU all...so much!!!

Harrison House, thank you for your love and grace and patience and for all the work you do to share the Word of God with all ages. Thank you for loving young people with your gifts and talents, causing them to grow and thrive and be established in the love of Jesus. God bless you all.

Love,
Cathy

table of contents

introduction

Dear Friend,

May I just begin by saying how honored I am to be part of your life in helping you to understand the most beautiful treasure God has given to us—prayer. What a privilege we have as God's daughters in that we get to pray. We get to spend time in conversation with the Lord Who created the entire universe, Who has made Himself available to us 24/7…365 days…every minute…every second of our lives throughout all eternity. We get to call on the name of the Lord and He hears us, helps us, leads us, guides us, corrects us, and loves us.

When we come to God with all of our heart, soul, mind, and strength, absolutely know that we are going to hear from Him. Through prayer we can and will have an opportunity to bring healing and restoration to many others along with ourselves.

Have you ever wondered if someone ever has prayed for you? Just in case you think no one has ever prayed for you, I'm going to tell you that I have prayed for you and will continue. Even though I may not know you in person, I consider you my spiritual daughter and count it a great honor and responsibility to pray for you as I am writing to you.

My heart so much wants you to know and experience the presence of God in your life like never before. As you read this *little pink book*, I long for you to see how much God loves you, how much He wants to hear from you, and how much He cares about everything that concerns you. He also wants to speak to you. He wants to put real, true, pure faith in your heart as you read and hear His Word. As you worship Him and thank Him, I pray that you will forever know nothing can separate you from His love and His faithfulness to see you through every single circumstance in your life.

My prayer for you, my little sister, is that your life is graced with the wisdom and knowledge of an everlasting, loving, heavenly Father Who gave you His one and only Son so that He could have a relationship with you and call you His daughter. Oh, how His heart is set on yours—longing for you to delight in Him so you can enjoy the life He has given you.

As we turn the pages of this book together, let's allow these prayers and devotions to be a reminder that we don't have to, but we get to spend time with the Lord forever and ever. Amen.

With all my love and prayers,
Cathy

P.S.   Say this with me:

I get to worship and He loves me!

I get to pray and He hears me!

I get to read God's Word and He gives me understanding!

think pink

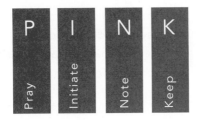

P — Pray
I — Initiate
N — Note
K — Keep

JOHN 3:16 AMP

For God so greatly loved and dearly prized the world that He [even] gave up His only begotten (unique) Son, so that whoever believes in (trusts in, clings to, relies on) Him shall not perish (come to destruction, be lost) but have eternal (everlasting) life.

what's a girl to do?

So what's a girl to do when she feels like her heart has been cracked wide open for the whole world to see?

How about when she's trying to figure out her future?

What about when she's had the biggest fight ever with her dad or mom?

What if she wants so badly to help someone but doesn't know how?

What if her best friend has told a lie about her just to make herself look good?

Can you relate to any of these scenarios?

When my husband Blaine and I got married, we began from the get-go ministering to children. I remember a little ditty we use to teach the kids that went like this: "Read your Bible, pray every-day, and you'll grow...grow...grow."[1] You may remember that song too and although it's a simple little song, oh what a powerful message to put into practice in our lives.

What is a girl to do?

I would have to say let's read our Bible and pray everyday. Reading God's Word and putting it in our hearts is one of the best ways to learn to pray, and praying God's Word is such an effective way to pray. When we pray God's Word we are in agreement with everything God has promised us and asked us to do. It keeps us in line with His truth and His heart.

One of my prayers for you is that as you read this *little pink book* and as you pray these prayers, you'll begin to pray, knowing like never before that the Lord backs up His Word for you, His daughter.

beauty

Father,

Today I say boldly that I am Your workmanship, created in Christ Jesus for good works.[2] You created me and made me to be the young lady that I am today. Your love and joy makes me beautiful on the inside, for I know according to Romans 5:5, the love of God has been shed generously abroad in my heart. As I allow that love to come out of me, so does Your goodness and beauty in my world!

Thank You for the appearance I have been given—my eyes, my ears, my nose, my face, my hair, and my entire body. You said in the Scriptures my body is the temple and dwelling place of the Holy Spirit.[3] Therefore, just as the priests of the Old Testament took care of the Temple of God, I'm asking You to help me take very good care of this temple.

Please help me to accept, love, and honor myself today. I ask for strength when looking in the mirror; let me see how beautiful I am, inside and out. Let my light from within shine brightly for the world to see.

Father, today I remind myself of the words of the Apostle Paul to all Christians in 1 Thessalonians 5:23: "May God himself, the God of peace, sanctify you through and through. May your whole spirit, soul and body be kept blameless at the coming of our Lord Jesus Christ" (NIV). I know that You are coming soon and it is my desire to please You when You return for me.[4] Thank You for keeping me pure and without blame in the way I feed my heart and spirit, without blame in the things I allow to affect my mind and emotions, and without blame in the way I live for You in this body.[5]

Lord, no one can deny Your absolute wonder and beauty. Today I ask...be beautiful through me, in Jesus' name. Amen.

"When you understand who you are in Christ, a rest enters your soul that cannot coexist with striving and struggling. Just as darkness cannot coexist with light, striving for approval does not coexist with confidence in His grace. Who you are in Christ matters more than what you do. God accepts and loves you just as you are, to demonstrate His glory to all the world."[6]

—Darlene Zschech,
Singer and Songwriter

beauty

boldness

Dear Father God,

You said in the Bible that if I need anything I can just come ask You for it.[7] So I ask in the name of Jesus for boldness. God, please give me confidence to do everything You want me to do.

You said that I am the light of the world, so I pray that I set a great example of You with my friends, at school, with my family, and with everyone else I'm with.[8]

You also said in the Bible righteous people are as bold as lions![9] I know I'm righteous because of You, so I believe I am also bold. When I have a question or something important to say at school, I will be bold and raise my hand. When I'm hanging out with my friends, I will be bold to say and do things that please and honor You.

Father God, I know that fear is never from You, so I will not allow fear or timidity into my life. You've given me a spirit of power, and love, and self-discipline.[10] Because of Your strength and power in me, I'm confident, courageous, and fearless. I don't shrink back from difficulties, but instead I rise to challenges because I know that You live big in me. Things that seem impossible are possible with Your help.[11]

Also God, I pray that You help me to care more about what You think about me, than what other people might think about me. My goal is to please You. I'll be bold and very courageous, just like You tell me in the Bible to be.[12] I'm not intimidated by the plan You have for my life. With Your help, I'll do what You've called me to do. I will not back down. I will be bold every time I talk to You.

I don't ever have to be afraid to approach You because I know You have perfect love for me. No matter what I've ever done or might ever do, I know You're always there to love and forgive me. My confidence is in You, in Jesus name, amen.

what's a girl to do?
when she needs courage

For God has not given us a spirit of
fear, but of power and of love and of
a sound mind.

2 Timothy 1:7 NKJV

All of us have moments in life when we desperately need courage. It may be courage to face a new school where you don't know anyone, courage to try out for a position as a cheerleader or to play another sport, or simply to face each new day and its challenges.

For me, it was a fear of failure—that I wouldn't be good enough and people would laugh at me. But my fears were changed to courage and boldness when I realized what amazing things God had to say to me from His Word and when I began to speak them over myself: "I have strength for all things in Christ Who empowers me, [I am ready for anything and equal to anything through Him Who infuses inner strength into me; I am self-sufficient in Christ's sufficiency]" (Phil. 4:13 AMP). You can have courage that you can do all things through *Him*.

Every time fear tries to creep back in, no matter what your situation is, remember what His Word says, "be strong and brave. Don't ever be afraid or discouraged! I am the LORD your God, and I will be there to help you wherever you go" (Josh. 1:9 CEV). As daughters of God, fear will quickly dissolve when we turn our thoughts to what God's Word has to say, making His thoughts our thoughts instead of focusing on the situation and feelings of fear.

Take courage today. No matter what you are facing, God will give you courage when you ask Him for it!

think pink

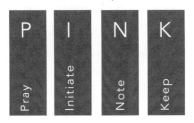

P	**I**	**N**	**K**
Pray	Initiate	Note	Keep

courage from God's Word

1 JOHN 4:16-18 NIV

God is love. Whoever lives in love lives in God, and God in him. In this way, love is made complete among us so that we will have confidence on the day of judgment, because in this world we are like him. There is no fear in love. But perfect love drives out fear, because fear has to do with punishment. The one who fears is not made perfect in love.

Rejoice in the Lord always. I will say it again: Rejoice! Let your gentleness be evident to all. The Lord is near. Do not be anxious about anything, but in everything, by prayer and petition, with thanksgiving, present your requests to God. And the peace of God, which transcends all understanding, will guard your hearts and your minds in Christ Jesus. Finally, brothers, whatever is true, whatever is noble, whatever is right, whatever is pure, whatever is lovely, whatever is admirable—if anything is excellent or praiseworthy—think about such things. Whatever you have learned or received or heard from me, or seen in me—put it into practice. And the God of peace will be with you.

Father,

I thank You that You said that Your perfect love would drive out all fear.[13] You have not given me a spirit of fear but instead You have placed in me a spirit of love and power and a sound mind.[14] You are near to me and I choose to talk to You and be thankful as I ask You for help. Thank You for guarding my heart and my mind as I turn my thoughts to You.[15] I receive Your peace because You are the God of peace.[16] As I think on good things and praise You, I know that Your courage is sure to rise up in me. Knowing how much You love me makes me confident to take on anything You ask of me. Thank You, thank You, in the mighty name of Jesus. Amen.

There is not in the world a kind of life more sweet and delightful than that of a continual conversation with God."17

—Brother Lawrence
17th Century Lay Minister

what's a girl to do?
when she needs creativity

God created the Heavens and
Earth—all you see, all you don't see…
God spoke: "Let us make human
beings in our image, make them
reflecting our nature…."

Genesis 1:1, 27 MSG

Lord, help me shine in…the arts.

From this moment on don't allow yourself to ever
say, "I am not creative."

I like to think of God as the "Master Artist." He did,
after all, create the entire universe and everything
in it! Think about how many different and unique
things there are in this universe. It's incredible—all
the different animals, plants, landscapes, colors,
sounds, tastes, and smells. Some of which maybe
you wish He hadn't created!

But most importantly, He created you and not a
single other person is exactly the same. What's
even cooler is the Master Artist, the One Who

created this entire amazing universe has placed that creativity inside of you! Genesis 1:27 (MSG) says, "God spoke: 'Let us make human beings in our image, make them reflecting our nature.'" That means we have God's creative nature in us too!

So next time you feel like you are no good in the arts or you are struggling to come up with an idea, just pray and thank God that His creativity can be shown through you. And now that you know you are the daughter of the "Master Artist" don't allow yourself to ever say, "I am not creative."

creativity

Father,

You are the Creator of the universe and all of the incredible and beautiful things in it. I thank You, the Master Artist, and am humbled You have placed that same creativity inside of me! I ask that every day You help me to realize it is not by my own efforts but with Your help that I can shine with extraordinary creativity in the arts. Take my hands, Lord, and use them to create amazing things that will bring honor to You, in Jesus' name. Amen.

wising up

Do you see a man wise in his own eyes? There is more hope for a fool than for him.

Proverbs 26:12 NIV

The Lord warns us not to be wise in our own eyes because our hope dims when that happens. What exactly does this mean? A person who is wise in their own eyes is a person who has taken their eyes off the Lord and onto themselves. This is called pride. Pride basically says that we can do things by ourself without God's help. The best way to avoid pride is to take time to pray and to meditate on the Word of God. By doing this, we are admitting we cannot navigate life alone; we must have the Lord's strength and direction. Take a moment today and tell the Lord how much you need Him. Remind Him that without His wisdom and guidance, you are hopeless.

Now ask Him to speak to you, to lead you, and to encourage you.[19] He has promised to do all of that!

Dear God,

Thank You so much for the life that You have given me. You are so good to me, and I want to trust You with every part of my life. I know You love me and I ask You to help me realize just how much You really do care about me.

You said in Jeremiah 29:11 that You've given me a great future. In Psalm 23:6, You said goodness and mercy will follow me every day of my life, and favor will surround me everywhere I go! And in Romans 8:28, You even promised to take the messed up parts of my life and turn those around for good.

When life gets tough and bad things happen, I absolutely know the bad things are not from You. You said in the Bible that You only do wondrous things. I know You are good, and every good thing is from You.[20] It's the devil who wants to steal, and kill, and destroy things in my life. But You, Father God, only want the absolute best for me.[21] *God please help me to always keep Your perspective on life. I won't blame You if life gets difficult. I'll just lean in closer to You because I know that You love me so much. Help me not to freak out about little things that really don't matter in life, and also help me to take the important things seriously.*

God, I've made a decision to live for You and I will stick it out until the very end. I want to fulfill the plan You have for me. I pray in Jesus' name that nothing will hinder or stop me from doing all that You've called me to do. Help me to show more people how wonderful You are.

I pray I will accurately represent You to everyone around me. I won't be flaky and religious, but I also won't be ashamed of You in any way.

Thank You, Father, that You promised to always lead and guide me through life.[22] Because I am submitted to You, You are directing every one of my footsteps.[23] You said in the Bible You won't ever leave me alone. You even said You'll go ahead of me in life and prepare the way for me to go.[24] You have the answers to all the questions I have about my life. Help me, Lord, to stay sensitive to Your voice and always make the best decisions in life.

I choose to trust You, and I choose not to worry. I give You every care and concern about my destiny. Thanks for planning in advance great things for me to do in Jesus' name, amen.[25]

eternity

Yet God has made everything beautiful for its own time. He has planted eternity in the human heart, but even so, people cannot see the whole scope of God's work from beginning to end.

Ecclesiastes 3:11 NLT

In this verse, your Father is telling you that you can never be fully satisfied with worldly things or worldly success. He created you in His image and *eternity has been planted in your heart*. In Psalm 139:13, 15, and 16, He tells you that He made all the delicate, inner parts of your body and knit them together in your mother's womb. He was there while you were being formed in utter seclusion. He saw you before you were born and scheduled each day of your life before you began to breathe. Every day was recorded in His Book! Your heavenly Father has had you on His mind since before you were even conceived. He will have you on His mind for all eternity.

my destiny

In the *Amplified Bible* it is said this way: "He also has planted eternity in men's hearts and minds [a divinely implanted sense of a purpose working through the ages which nothing under the sun but God alone can satisfy]." Your Father created a special place in your heart just for His Holy Spirit to fill. Nothing else fits that special spot. You may have felt a sense of emptiness or loneliness that you tried to fill with all kinds of worldly pleasures, but there isn't anything that you can cram into that spot that will complete you, except the eternal God.

You have made the wisest choice you will ever make by inviting Him to fill that special spot in your heart with His presence. The Bible tells you He'll never leave you nor forsake you.[18] Make another wise choice—don't ever leave Him or forsake Him!

thank you Lord for my '66 chevy

I have a lot of fond memories growing up in Canada. I know I'm going to sound like an old lady to you as I start handing out dates but here we go. I was born in 1961 and have so many wonderful recollections of winter. One in particular was going to driver's school. My dad thought it would be a good idea for me to take my driving lessons in the dead of winter. Looking back now, it makes a lot of sense. We had a good dose of winter up there and I needed to learn to drive on those snowy, slushy, icy streets.

I'm not sure what the legal age to drive is now, but when I was a kid we were able to get our learner's permit at fourteen. Well, I don't know about you, but I could hardly wait to drive and I drove from time to time with my parents for two years before I was sixteen. My birthday is in January so you better believe as soon as I could, I went down there to that Alberta driver's license office so confident but left there without my license—a little discouraged to say the least. My mom encouraged me and said we'd give it another go the next week.

So we did and can you believe it, I blew it again. I can't remember if it was that darn parallel parking or I may have gone through a stop sign. No matter what, I do remember a lot of tears that time and wondering if I'd ever get my license.

I recall having to wait about a month before I tried again, and this time I practiced every chance I got and really took it to prayer. As I was praying I remember thinking about all the reasons I wanted to drive. I have to admit, that whole feeling of independence was at the top of my list but I also got to thinking about how God had been so good to me over the last few years and how many times He provided rides for me anywhere I needed to go. Of course my dad and mom furnished most of those rides, whether they took me to dancing lessons, the movies, the mall, or anywhere else I needed or even wanted to go to. I also had some friends that were a little older and they were always so kind to give me a ride to church or football games.

So when I was praying, the Lord brought to mind when I got my license to always be generous in giving other people a lift when they needed it. I committed to Him I would do that and I really had a lot of opportunities. One thing I asked the Lord was to help me fill up my car for church and youth meetings and He always did.

I did a little driving for my dad and mom, too, when my brother and sister needed rides. I admit my attitude wasn't always the best. Years later I remember asking them to forgive me for being a grumpy sister at times and wishing they would start driving.

I was very blessed to have a car when I turned sixteen. It was a car that my parents had gotten from my grandparents—a red '66 Chevy Impala with a white roof. I'll never forget that long car with its gigantic steering wheel. The greatest thing was it held a lot of people and my dad put an eight track player in it for me. You probably don't know what that even is so just know it played all my favorite music. I was very proud of it and so thankful to the Lord and my dad and mom for giving me that car. I loved driving and still do to this day.

I'll never forget how excited I was for all three of my boys to get their drivers licenses. They are all two years apart and were all very excited to drive. I could so much relate. I took them each for their driving tests and we had a little tradition of going out for a great breakfast celebration the morning they got their license. Unlike me, they all got it on their first try; I was so happy for them. I think I was even more excited than they were.

Let me say as a mom, when my boys started to drive, as much as driver's school had taught them and their dad and I had taught them, I was thankful to know our faith was in God to continue to give them wisdom and protection and He has.

As you are preparing for that big day or maybe you already have your license, just remember that your heavenly Father is so wanting you to trust Him to help you. He is with you wherever you go. Let Him direct you. Listen to Him. Getting to drive is a privilege and with that comes responsibility. Driving can be a tool not only to get you from point A to point B but also to help others like your friends, your brothers and sisters, and your parents—even your own kids one day.

Sometimes I still get in my car and say, "Thank you, Father, that I get to drive," and I've been doing it for over thirty years. It's one of those things I try not to ever take for granted.

Something my husband and I are always thankful for are our vehicles. We've had many over the years and we know it has been the Lord Who has been so faithful to provide us with whatever we are driving. He will do the same for you. I was so fortunate to have my first car given to me, but over the years I have heard one young person after another tell of the wonderful ways the Lord helped them to get their first vehicle. God cares so much about whatever it is you need, so make sure you acknowledge Him and He will absolutely grace you with His help and favor. Nothing is too hard for God and when it comes to helping you, His daughter, He wants to give you wisdom in the steps to take. He's got a plan just for you and is just waiting to let you in on it. Let's let our requests be known and let's take a listen.

PINK PRAYER

driving

Father,

Thank You for being interested in every part of my life. I know that driving is a big deal and I don't take it lightly. I ask You to help me to prepare the best way I can by being diligent to study, practice, and pay attention in classes. Please help my parents to put their faith in You and not worry. I'm excited to be independent but also looking forward to using my driving as a gift to be available for others. I believe You'll lead me where I'm needed.

I want to say in faith thank You for providing me with a car. I am ready to do whatever You tell me. Show me the steps to take in finding the right car and direct me to the best place with the best prices. I will seek wise counsel before I buy a car and as I take these steps, I know You are a good shepherd and Father and I hear your voice.[26]

Help me to be patient when I drive and to bring You honor on the road and off. I am so thankful and excited for this new season of my life, in Jesus' name. Amen.

think pink

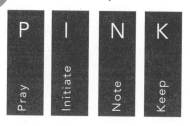

P Pray
I Initiate
N Note
K Keep

When you get your license, every once in a while take a little time to drive somewhere with your parents. I know for years and years I drove and drove and drove my boys all over the place. I'm sorry to say, I sometimes complained but now that they are all grow up, one of my favorite things to do is drive somewhere with them—even if we just get a coffee, drive around, and have a nice chat. I don't even care who drives, I just love spending time with my boys. It can be nice for you too.

why pray for my enemies?

Love your enemies, bless those who curse you, do good to those who hate you, and pray for those who spitefully use you and persecute you.

Matthew 5:44 NKJV

Let's do this because Jesus said to!

You and I both know it's not easy to pray for anyone who has mistreated us. I know I sure don't feel like doing that, but let's choose to do what Jesus says rather than what we feel like doing.

When we choose to bless someone, especially when we want to do the opposite, we are choosing to keep our hearts tender and pure and there's no telling what the Lord can do in our circumstances. He will do wonderful things in our lives and in the lives of the people we are praying for!

As I was reading through Proverbs, this particular verse stood out to me: "Do not say, 'I'll pay you back for this wrong!' Wait for the LORD, and he will deliver you" (Prov. 20:22 NIV).

All of us have been wronged by people—perhaps a friend, a co-worker, a family member, or the person in traffic yesterday! You see, we have all had things done or said to us that have hurt from time to time. The answer is never to try to get even. Our justice is always the wrong answer.

We will fail when we try to deliver ourselves, but when we pray for our enemies and simply wait on the Lord for deliverance and justice, it will come—in His way and His time. And remember, God is more concerned with blessing you than He is in judging your betrayer.

Let's take a moment today to forgive and pray for our enemies—those who may have hurt you, either intentionally or not.

Father,

It is not up to me to get even today. You never desired to get even with me when I wronged You, misused Your name, or simply ignored Your hand of goodness in my life. Today, I pray for those who have wronged me, used me, betrayed me, and left me. Please show Your love to them and bring them close to You. I forgive, even if I can't always forget. And Lord, when I do remember, I will forgive again, just as you have forgiven me.[29]

In the name of your Son, Jesus, who had the worst enemies and displayed the greatest mercy. Amen.

what's a girl to do?
when she needs favor

Have you ever known someone who just seems to be friends with everyone? Maybe you've tried to act and talk a certain way to get people to like you? Or have you ever had to beg and plead for something you really wanted?

Saying and doing the right things to get what you want may work for a while, but it's exhausting! The problem is you have to keep saying and doing the right things to keep those friendships or to eventually get what you have been asking and begging for.

So how do you gain the approval of others, or finally get what you've been asking and begging for?

It's called God's favor and it comes effortlessly.

Favor is basically God working to make things happen for you that might not normally happen, or blessing us with things we might not normally receive, just because He loves us. For example, maybe you have really wanted a new pair of shoes or a new shirt and you just don't have enough money for it. The next time you go to the store, you look and see that it is 50% off and you now have just enough to buy it! Or maybe you just moved to a new school and really want to make new friends but don't know how. God's favor can cause people to like you who normally would never be friends with you.

Favor is a free gift from God, so if we ask and believe, we will have it. Psalms 5:12 (NIV) says, "For surely, O LORD, you bless the righteous; you surround them with your favor as with a shield."

What have you been trying to do in your own efforts that you need God's favor for? Ask Him today.

favor

Father,

Thank You for Your favor in my life today. I believe You are working behind the scenes to bring about new friendships and opportunities that might not normally be available. Thank You for favor with my parents, teachers, and everyone I come in contact with each day. And thank You Father for giving me favor even with the things I've been asking for, no matter how big or small, in Jesus' name. Amen.

Remember, good old fashioned manners go a long way. Doing to others as you would have them do to you will surely bring favor. Good manners are really a form of love, respect, and consideration for others. They will help you shine in all your relationships.

think pink

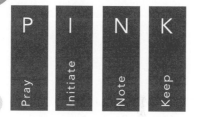

The Teen Creed

Don't let your parents down
They brought you up

Be humble enough to obey
You may give orders someday

Choose companions with care
You become what they are

Guard your thoughts
What you think, you are

Choose only a date
Who would make a good mate

Be master of your habits
Or they will master you

Don't be a show off when you drive,
Drive with safety and arrive

Don't let the crowd pressure you,
Stand for something or you'll
    fall for anything.[30]

—Author Unknown

Lord,

There are times that I feel like giving up—times I feel like I'm never going to fully accomplish the things that I have set my heart after. But today, I make a choice not to allow my feelings and emotions to be the deciding factor of what I do each day. Your Word tells me that I should walk by faith and not by what I see and feel.[31] I chose to do that today.

I ask You to supply me with the full measure of grace and the spirit of perseverance to develop a finisher's heart. You have told me in Galatians 6:9, "Let's not get tired of doing what is good, for at the right time we will reap a harvest-if we do not give up" (ISV). In the name of Jesus, I will not tire, I will not quit, and I will not retreat from doing what is good. I will do good things to both my friends and my enemies. I will do good work in my assignments. I will do what is right in my walk with You each day.

And Lord, I really do believe that my harvest is coming because I will not faint or give up. As I run this race, I am keeping my eyes on Jesus, Who for the joy that was set before Him, endured the cross, scorning its shame and is now seated at the right hand of God. Jesus is my example. He never quit on me. He went all the way to the cross, rose from the dead, and completed His assignment.

Jesus had a finisher's heart and His Spirit has come to live in me, giving me the heart of a finisher as well![32] Thank You Father that I can see the finish line—fulfilling Your will for me—and I will not be denied my destiny.

In the enduring, eternal name above all names, Jesus. Amen.

both sides of forgiveness

Forgiving others is always easier when we remember that God has forgiven us and loves us when we've blown it. What a gift and what joy it brings to us when we receive the forgiveness Jesus has provided for us.[33] Have you ever known the forgiveness of a friend or family member when you've let them down? Boy-oh-boy, I sure have and how thankful I am to be free from the guilt and shame, and to be given a fresh start from them and the Lord.

The Lord will give us the strength and the courage to ask forgiveness and also to give forgiveness. It only takes a moment to make the choice—the right choice. I have to say, forgiveness changes everything for you and me, and others, too.

When we choose to obey what Jesus has asked us to do, it's a beautiful thing to see Him do His part—only something He can do. He washes us as white as snow like only He can.[34] I grew up in western Canada and what a sight to see a lovely fresh snowfall. Everything is so clean and sparkly. I was just up there a few weeks ago and forgot how important it is to have my sunglasses on when I'm driving. There is such a glare on a sunny day when you're on the road. All I can say is I just love it.

Even when it's hard to ask for forgiveness and swallow our pride or when it's tough to forgive some one else, just remember either way we're going to shine. Our willingness to receive God's forgiveness is so important because as we taste and see how good it is, our cup will overflow to give it to others.

This Christian life we live is so much about forgiving and being forgiven. Did you realize that Jesus even told us in the book of Mark that we need to forgive one another so God can forgive us?[35] I'd say forgiveness is a priority in our relationships. Jesus wants us free from all bitterness and resentment. He wants our hearts to remain tender and loving so we can be free, then He can touch others through us.

P.S. Remember to forgive yourself, too, and go on. When we ask the Lord to forgive us, He does and He forgets it. How far is the east from the west? That's how far God takes our sin away from us (Psalm 103:2).

forgiveness

Father,

Thank You for Your forgiveness in my life. I ask You to help me to forgive others. Help me to forgive over and over and over again just like You said in Luke 17:3. You have put Your love in my heart and I want to be like You in showing Your mercy, grace, and forgiveness. I choose to obey Your commands and not go by my feelings. When I don't feel like forgiving I know You have the best in mind for me. I trust You and will always keep in mind all You have done for me.

Thank You Lord, through You, I'm a girl who forgives and is forgiven, in Jesus' name. Amen.

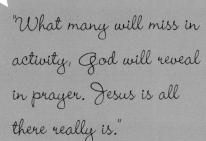

"What many will miss in activity, God will reveal in prayer. Jesus is all there really is."

—Anne Murchinson

Wife of Clint Murchinson Jr., Founder of the Dallas Cowboys

friction

As iron sharpens iron, so one man sharpens another.

Proverbs 27:17 NIV

I would like to share a couple thoughts on the verse above. You know, when iron rubs against iron it does not make a soothing sound and there is some pretty good friction created in the process. Iron on iron is not sweet, cuddly, and precious—you get the point!

In order to grow as Christians, we all need friends and mentors in our life who will rub up against us with truth, discernment, and counsel that leaves us sharper when it's all over. That is not to say friends can't be a lot of fun most of the time, but in order for a friendship to go deep, we have to be willing to bare our hearts, and have give and take when it comes to life and spiritual growth.

My challenge to you is to find or begin to create that kind of friendship. If you have a good

Christian friend already, next time you get together, dare to ask a couple questions like this:

"Tell me what the Lord has been showing you or doing in your life lately?"

"Is there anything you see in my life God wants to refine and improve?"

Let's give permission in our close and trusted relationships to go deeper and let Jesus work in us to do His will and good pleasure.[36]

think pink

P I N K

Pray | Initiate | Note | Keep

relationships God's way

God gives us lots of ideas on how to keep great relationships with parents, siblings, friends, co-workers. His Word is there to help us when we don't know how to deal with other people. When we pray for others, it's a supernatural link—a connection to God on behalf of those we care about and well, even those we struggle with. When you bring people before the Lord in prayer, you'll see amazing changes.

friendships

When it comes to friends, it's up to you to decide who you let walk away, who you let stay, and who you refuse to let go. Stay open to God's still, small voice inside that clues you in to which friends you should keep close. Remember: When you choose your friends, you are actually choosing your future. Don't settle for anything less than God's best for you.

for friends

Father God,

Bless all my friends in whatever it is that You know they may need this day! And may their lives be full of your peace, prosperity, and power as they seek to have a closer relationship with You. Help me to be a blessing to them. In Proverbs 18:24, Your Word says there is a friend who sticks closer than a brother (or sister). Connect me to friends like that and help me to be a true friend in return, in Jesus' name, Amen.

grace for the race

Wherefore seeing we also are compassed about with so great a cloud of witnesses, let us lay aside every weight, and the sin which doth so easily beset us, and let us run with patience the race that is set before us, looking unto Jesus....

Hebrews 12:1-2

In each of our lives, there is a "besetting" sin that can tower like a mountain between us and God. This is "the sin which doth so easily beset us" and it differs according to the person. What a besetting sin is to one person may not trouble another at all. Sometimes this sin is quite obvious to others, while in other cases it is hidden in the heart and known only to the individual and God. In either case, it is perplexing and harassing, and, if allowed to linger and grow, it may end in tragic moral failure. Practically every believer wrestles with a habitually assaulting sin, even those who appear to be very strong believers.

The word *beset* means to "surround."[37] This sin is like an army: it tries to surrounds us, and continually attacks us from every side. We don't have to look for it; somehow, it just finds us.

The Bible give us examples of this in Moses, with his explosive temper, and David, with his lust for women.[38] These devoted men of God walked humbly and persistently in the will of God, but when they grew weak in faith and weary in their warfare against evil, a besetting sin reared up its ugly head to challenge them. Fortunately, they both knew the only way to overcome was to run to God when they fell, and they cried out for His help. A besetting sin can either drive us closer to God or drive us away from God. We must make the right choice.

The first step in conquering a besetting sin is to know who you really are. You must remember that you are a born again child of God who has been given a new heart with new desires. Never take on the identity of a temptation that you are struggling with. Just because a person has lustful desires to be with the same sex does not make them a homosexual. If you had a temptation to commit sexual sin with the opposite sex, you would never label yourself a "fornicator," would you? If you are tempted to take something that isn't yours, that does not make you a thief. When you know who you are, it will change the way you act.

This is precisely why this verse concludes with, "looking unto Jesus." Get your eyes on Jesus and His love for you. He is the one who gives each of us the power and grace to conquer any sinful habit.

growing the fruit of the Spirit

When we receive Jesus as the Lord of our life, something miraculous happens in that His Spirit is in us. He has filled us with something precious called the fruit of the Spirit. I say precious because we need this fruit every hour of our lives. It is vital that we take care of it just like you care for a garden. The Lord has gently placed nine fruits in us and desires to see every one of these grow in our lives. Galatians 5:22–23 says the fruit of the Spirit is love, joy, peace, patience, kindness, goodness, faithfulness, gentleness and self-control.

Growing fruit takes time. The fact is growing to be more like Jesus takes time too. I really believe the more we spend time focusing on God and others, we will see these fruits grow in our lives. As we reach out, the Spirit of God is working in us and through us. Really, the more we practice these loving character traits, the more evident they'll become in our lives. With God's grace, we can produce a bountiful harvest.

think pink

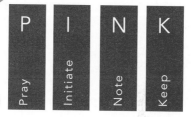

P — Pray

I — Initiate

N — Note

K — Keep

for the fruit of the Spirit

GALATIANS 5:22-23

NIV

But the fruit of the Spirit is love, joy, peace, patience, kindness, goodness, faithfulness, gentleness and self-control.

Father,

Thank You for Your Son, Jesus. I know I have eternal life because I believe in Him. I believe nothing can separate me from Your love. You did not give me a spirit of fear, but a spirit of power, of love, and of self-discipline. I will love others as You love me and I determine to love those with whom I live, attend school, and meet with each day. And most of all, Lord, help me to love You with all my heart and with all my soul and with all my mind. In the name of Jesus, amen.

think pink

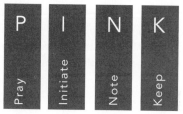

love scriptures

For God so loved the world that he gave his one and only Son, that whoever believes in him shall not perish but have eternal life.

John 3:16 NIV

Who shall separate us from the love of Christ? Shall trouble or hardship or persecution or famine or nakedness or danger or sword...neither height nor depth, nor anything else in all creation, will be able to separate us from the love of God that is in Christ Jesus our Lord.

Romans 8:35, 39 niv

For God did not give us a spirit of timidity, but a spirit of power, of love and of self-discipline.

2 Timothy 1:7 niv

My command is this: Love each other as I have loved you...This is my command: Love each other.

John 15:12, 17 niv

Jesus replied: "Love the Lord your God with all your heart and with all your soul and with all your mind."

Matthew 22:37 niv

Every Teen Girl's Little Pink Book

joy

Father God,

Thank you for putting Your life in me; thank You for filling me with joy by Your presence; thank You that I can know eternal pleasures as I live my life in and for You. I am loving my new life in You and the fact that You delight in me; I am thankful for peace in my heart; I am amazed You rejoice over me with Your song of love. I draw on Your joy to give me strength for this day and all it holds. I count it all joy, all strength, when I experience tests and trials because I know by Your Word that I have strength for all things in You, in Jesus' name. Amen.

think pink

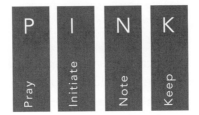

P — Pray
I — Initiate
N — Note
K — Keep

joy scriptures

You have made known to me the path of life; you will fill me with joy in your presence, with eternal pleasures at your right hand.

Psalm 16:11 NIV

The LORD your God is with you, he is mighty to save. He will take great delight in you, he will quiet you with his love, he will rejoice over you with singing.

Zephaniah 3:17 NIV

Consider it pure joy, my brothers, whenever you face trials of many kinds, because you know that the testing of your faith develops perseverance.

James 1:2-3 NIV

...for the joy of the LORD is your strength.

Nehemiah 8:10 NIV

peace

Father,

Thank You for great peace because I am learning to love Your Word and use it in my daily life. I do desire to please You by my way of life, causing my enemies to live at peace with me. I choose to receive the peace You have for me so my heart is not troubled or afraid. I guard my mind with Your Word so it is controlled by the Spirit of life and peace. Your peace You give to me passes my natural understanding and guards my heart and mind in Christ Jesus. I will be a peacemaker and raise up a harvest of righteousness in my life. Amen.

think pink

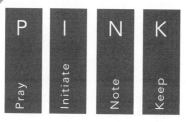

P — Pray
I — Initiate
N — Note
K — Keep

peace scriptures

Great peace have they who love your law,
and nothing can make them stumble.

Psalm 119:165 NIV

When a man's ways are pleasing to the
LORD, he makes even his enemies live
at peace with him.

Proverbs 16:7 NIV

Peace I leave with you; my peace I give you. I do not give to you as the world gives. Do not let your hearts be troubled and do not be afraid.

John 14:27 NIV

The mind of sinful man is death, but the mind controlled by the Spirit is life and peace.

Romans 8:6 NIV

And the peace of God, which transcends all understanding, will guard your hearts and your minds in Christ Jesus.

Philippians 4:7 NIV

Peacemakers who sow in peace raise a harvest of righteousness.

James 3:18 NIV

patience

Thank You, my Father,

For helping me to remain completely humble and gentle in my behavior and attitudes; being patient and bearing with my family and friends in all situations that come up each day. Thank You for strengthening me with Your power according to Your glorious might, so that I can exhibit great endurance and patience, joyfully.

think pink

patience scriptures

Be completely humble and gentle; be patient, bearing with one another in love.

Ephesians 4:2 NIV

...being strengthened with all power according to his glorious might so that you may have great endurance and patience....

Colossians 1:11 NIV

kindness

Dear Lord,

Thank you for showing Your rich grace, which is expressed in Your kindness, to me. I am Your chosen child, loved and dressed in Your compassion and kindness, with humility, gentleness, and patience being developed in me. Because of Your kindness and love, I received new life revealed in Your mercy. You washed me and renewed me and poured out Your Holy Spirit on me and in me because of what Jesus has done for me on the cross. Amen.

think pink

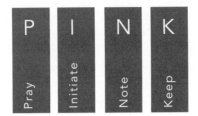

P I N K

Pray Initiate Note Keep

kindness scriptures

...in order that in the coming ages he might show the incomparable riches of his grace, expressed in his kindness to us in Christ Jesus.

Ephesians 2:7 NIV

Therefore, as God's chosen people, holy and dearly loved, clothe yourselves with compassion, kindness, humility, gentleness and patience.

Colossians 3:12 NIV

But when the kindness and love of God our Savior appeared, he saved us, not because of righteous things we had done, but because of his mercy. He saved us through the washing of rebirth and renewal by the Holy Spirit, whom he poured out on us generously through Jesus Christ our Savior.

Titus 3:4-6 NIV

Father,

Thank you for giving me confidence in knowing I will see Your goodness in my life. How great is Your goodness that You have stored up for me for this time, because I have committed my life to You and take my refuge in You daily. I am thankful for the riches of Your kindness, tolerance, and patience in my life. I know that it is because of Your kindness that I was drawn to come to repentance and newness of life in Christ Jesus. Amen.

think pink

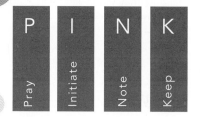

goodness scriptures

I am still confident of this: I will see the goodness of the LORD in the land of the living.

Psalm 27:13 NIV

How great is your goodness, which you have stored up for those who fear you, which you bestow in the sight of men on those who take refuge in you.

Psalm 31:19 NIV

Or do you show contempt for the riches of his kindness, tolerance and patience, not realizing that God's kindness leads you toward repentance?

Romans 2:4 NIV

faithfulness

Lord,

Thank You that I'm empowered through Christ with righteousness and faithfulness, and for rewarding me for the very things You've given me. Your amazing love reaches to the heavens and Your faithfulness to the skies. What a display of Your greatness in my world! I will speak of Your faithfulness and salvation and not conceal Your love and Your truth to those with whom I live, study, and play. I will faithfully love You and draw my strength from You, because Your faithfulness lasts forever.

think pink

P — Pray
I — Initiate
N — Note
K — Keep

faithfulness scriptures

The LORD rewards every man for his righteousness and faithfulness.

1 Samuel 26:23 NIV

Your love, O LORD, reaches to the heavens, your faithfulness to the skies.

Psalm 36:5 NIV

I do not hide your righteousness in my heart; I speak of your faithfulness and salvation. I do not conceal your love and your truth from the great assembly.

Psalm 40:10 NIV

My faithful love will be with him, and through my name his horn will be exalted.

Psalm 89:24 NIV

Your faithfulness continues through all generations; you established the earth, and it endures.

Psalm 119:90 NIV

Father God,

I am blessed with Your wisdom which is pure, peace loving, always gentle, and willing to yield to others. Because Your wisdom is gentle in me, mercy and good deeds are born through me, playing no favorites and done sincerely. Your gentleness has the capacity to make me great through Your love. As Your servant, I endeavor not to quarrel or be contentious, but to gently and patiently lead others in humility.

think pink

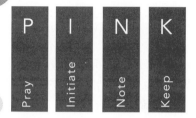

P I N K

Pray Initiate Note Keep

gentleness scriptures

But the wisdom from above is first of all pure. It is also peace loving, gentle at all times, and willing to yield to others. It is full of mercy and good deeds. It shows no favoritism and is always sincere.

James 3:17 NLT

You have also given me the shield of Your salvation; Your gentleness has made me great.

2 Samuel 22:36 NKJV

And a servant of the Lord must not quarrel but be gentle to all, able to teach, patient....

2 Timothy 2:24 NKJV

They must not slander anyone and must avoid quarreling. Instead, they should be gentle and show true humility to everyone.

Titus 3:2 NLT

self-control

Father,

Because of all the fruit of the Spirit being nurtured in me through Your Word, which is Truth, I am making every effort to add to my faith, goodness; and to goodness, knowledge; and to knowledge, self-control; and to self-control, perseverance; and to perseverance, godliness; and to godliness, brotherly kindness; and to brotherly kindness, love, in Jesus' name. Amen.

think pink

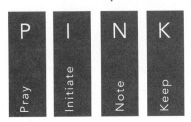

self-control scriptures

For this very reason, make every effort to add to your faith goodness; and to goodness, knowledge; and to knowledge, self-control; and to self-control, perseverance; and to perseverance, godliness; and to godliness, brotherly kindness; and to brotherly kindness, love.

2 Peter 1:5-7 NIV

We have not received the spirit of the world but the Spirit who is from God, that we may understand what God has freely given us.

1 Corinthians 2:12 NIV

"Do the thing that you think you cannot do."

—Eleanor Roosevelt

First Lady of the United States of America

goals

Becky, a dear friend of mine, recently trained for and completed a whole triathlon. I asked her to write about it because I thought you would be as inspired as I was when she told me she was doing it. I am so proud of her and I know this story will challenge you to have big dreams and goals. God will be right there alongside, helping you to accomplish what He has put in your heart to do.

triathlon

I have always been a fairly active person, but only if I could enjoy what I was doing and have fun while I was doing it. I never went too far outside my comfort zone. I was a swimmer in high school but usually goofed off during practices and never took it all too seriously.

This past year a friend of mine called to tell me they had finished a triathlon. I immediately thought, *Wow, that sounds incredible, I wish I could do one of those!* So over the course of the next few days my mind battled with the thoughts: *Why not do one? No, I'm not a good enough athlete. I could never...I'm not someone who could finish something like that! I'd just make a fool of myself in front of all of those people.*

So I was confronted with a choice, either live with the mentality I'd never be good enough, or decide to make a commitment to push myself farther than I had ever done before to accomplish my impossible. So I made the commitment. I signed up for the race, paid my money, and told my friends I was going to do a triathlon in five months!

Training was hard work but with all of my new excitement it was easy to stay motivated in the beginning. But as the weeks and months went by, I found the thoughts creeping back in: *What if I can't do it? What if I finish last?* As the thoughts came, I turned my attention to what God's Word said about me: "I can do everything through Christ, who gives me strength" (Phil. 4:13 NLT).

Race day came and sure enough, all of the training and commitment I made to my goal paid off.

I finished, and with a *huge* smile on my face! I had accomplished what was once my impossible.

What goals have you been afraid to take on? Is there a negative voice in you saying "Don't try, you might fail. You're not good enough, pretty enough, smart enough…?" I encourage you to stretch beyond your comfort zone; make a commitment to accomplish whatever might seem to be your impossible! Remember, you can do everything through Christ, who gives you strength!

Love,
Becky

"No man can follow Christ and go astray."

—William H. P. Faunce

Clergyman and Educator

what's a girl to do?
about the future

What do you want to be? Where are you going to go to college? What are you going to do for a job this summer? Do you feel like you are constantly being bombarded with questions?

Our culture is all about having a plan—having an answer and sounding like we have it all together. Of course it is important to think things through and to have vision for the future, but sometimes people can get so swept away in all the planning and effort to look successful, that they don't even make time to talk to God about it.

Don't get overwhelmed—just take things step by step. God wants you to use your mind when making decisions about your future. He wants you to seek counsel from people you trust. But most importantly, He wants you to surrender everything to Him. When He does lead you to take a step that doesn't seem the logical thing to do, you must trust Him above your own understanding. When you are faithful to take that step, in a few years you will look back and it will all make sense! God has good and amazing things for your future that begin with the steps you take in prayer today.

Proverbs 3:5-6 (CEV) says, "With all your heart you must trust the LORD and not your own judgment. Always let him lead you, and he will clear the road for you to follow."

when I don't
know what to do

Lord,

I acknowledge You in this step of my life. I trust in
You and not in my own understanding or abilities.
Show me what I should do and the steps I should
take at this time. Thank You for going before me
and making a way, in Jesus' name. Amen.

my future today

I will guide you and teach you the way
you should go. I will give you good
advice and watch over you.

Psalm 32:8 NIRV

God cares about your future. In fact, He knows
exactly what will make you the happiest and is
already working to help you bring it to pass. There
is something all of us need to remember and it's
found in Proverbs: "Where there is no revelation,
the people cast off restraint; but blessed is he who
keeps the law" (Prov. 29:18 NIV).

Now think about when the last time was God gave
you a revelation about your life or your future. Ask
yourself, "What does the Lord desire to reveal to
me today?"

This verse tells us that without a revelation, people
cast off restraint. Another translation says that
without a vision, the people of God will perish.[39]
Even as we met together with some of our church
staff team today, we talked about the importance

of having vision for where we are going as a church and as individuals. Without vision, a church will die and so will the hopes of a person.

Years ago, I saw an interesting Charlie Brown cartoon. In the first frame Charlie was shooting an arrow. In the next frame Charlie Brown shot the arrow into his fence. In the final frame Charlie is painting a bull's-eye around the arrow! This is how we ALL live life sometimes... we run so fast that we don't take time to clearly mark out our path and vision. We have no bull's-eye.

The Lord was encouraging me again today to think and pray about the days ahead, allowing Him to provide revelation of what I need to be "shooting for."

Let's pray together.

my future

Lord,

You know better than I do what my life is meant to be,[40] so I throw myself completely and totally into Your perfect will and plan for my life. Bring revelation into my heart of the steps I need to take today and each day to follow. As Your vision is continually revealed to me, I will discipline myself to do my part to complete my course.

Lord, thank You that You love me and have a great plan for my life. I love the fact that with You, there is always hope no matter what I feel like at any single moment, in the name of Jesus, my Shepherd and my Guide, Amen.

what's a girl to do?
get to know God

Dear Girlfriend,

This is a prayer that Paul prayed for his friends that I pray for you. Although we may not know each other, there is no distance in prayer and I wouldn't be writing this book if you weren't in my thoughts and in my heart. You can pray this prayer for yourself, your family, and friends too.

All through your Bible you will find wonderful prayers like this, and why wouldn't we want to pray prayers inspired by the Holy Spirit—prayers the heroes of the Bible spoke so earnestly out of their mouths?

God bless you, my lovely friend. I believe this prayer will be made real in your life as God begins to reveal Himself to you. I do love you and see you as a beautiful young woman who has a heart after Jesus.

With All My Heart,
Cathy xox

knowing God

"I have not stopped thanking God for you. I pray for you constantly, asking God, the glorious Father of our Lord Jesus Christ, to give you spiritual wisdom and insight so that you might grow in your knowledge of God. I pray that your hearts will be flooded with light so that you can understand the confident hope he has given to those he called—his holy people who are his rich and glorious inheritance.

"I also pray that you will understand the incredible greatness of God's power for us who believe him. This is the same mighty power that raised Christ from the dead and seated him in the place of honor at God's right hand in the heavenly realms. Now he is far above any ruler or authority or power or leader or anything else—not only in this world but also in the world to come. God has put all things under the authority of Christ and has made him head over all things for the benefit of the church. And the church is his body; it is made full and complete by Christ, who fills all things everywhere with himself" (Eph. 1:16-23 NLT).

full-on grace

Grace to you...my little girlfriend. I want to share something my husband, Blaine, wrote and I pray it blesses you as it has me:

In all my years of being a follower Jesus, I had never completely understood the grace of God. I had sung "Amazing Grace" a thousand times, but couldn't remember it really being taught about in church.

I think there are some things that prevent us from really experiencing the power of full-on grace. First, it seems in life, we are always keeping score. You have winners and losers in every game. All that matters is how well you played— did you measure up, did you win?

Secondly, the church has in many ways fallen into a climate of performance based Christianity. How long did you pray? How many chapters of the Bible did you read this week? Are you living a perfect Christian life? You get the picture. Our value in the church and with

God rises and falls based on how many rabbits we can pull out of the hat for God. Don't get me wrong, I think we all need to follow after the Lord with all our hearts and be passionate about living our faith. But I also think it's time to quit trying to count how many notches up or down we are with God.

I've thrown myself on the grace of God. God loves me in the good, the bad, and the ugly. And you know what? That makes me love Him even more. I have nothing to prove and no one to fear. I remind myself of the words of the Apostle Paul every day, "But by the grace of God I am what I am, and His grace toward me was not in vain; but I labored more abundantly than they all, yet not I, but the grace of God which was with me" (1 Cor. 15:10 NKJV).

I've actually come to believe that I will accomplish more by grace and humility, than by priding myself in checking off a list of spiritual rules and quotas. Don't worry; I still have goals and ambitions like anyone else. I still keep the score when I play a game with my boys, but today, everything begins from the staging ground of grace.

It starts every morning by getting up and knowing that God can't love me any more than He does right now. And He will never love me any less. And it's not a cheap, greasy, "get away with all you can" grace. It's a grace that cost Christ His very life and moves me to a deeper surrender everyday.

Lord,

Thank you today for the free, unearned gift of salvation. There was nothing I did to earn my relationship with You and there is nothing I can do to earn the right to keep it. You have loved me in spite of my messes and failures and Your love provokes me to serve You because I truly desire to, not because I have to.

Right now, I fall on Your grace...Your goodness...Your unconditional and unending love. Now please allow the grace you've shown me to find its way out of my heart and into the lives of those around me. Use me to shower down goodness and blessing to the people I meet today, that they may see You, in Jesus' name, amen.

being you is best!

All believers, come here and listen, let me tell you what God did for me. I called out to him with my mouth, my tongue shaped the sounds of music. If I had been cozy with evil, the Lord would never have listened. But he most surely did listen, he came on the double when he heard my prayer. Blessed be God: he didn't turn a deaf ear, he stayed with me, loyal in his love.

Psalm 66:16-20 msg

I remember listening to people pray, and feeling like I had to pray like they did. I always felt as if I didn't know enough to pray or what words I was even supposed to say. Should I walk, sit, bow, fold my hands, or should I end saying Jesus' name? Many have expressed this same concern when it comes to prayer.

When I think about prayer, I think about David who wrote most of the Psalms. God said that David was "a man after his own heart."[41]

This is encouraging for us; there is someone with God's heart of prayer we can learn from. David loved to write music, sing, play music or have it played, dance, and even get away from all the craziness of life to withdraw to a quiet place. This is exactly what we see in David's prayers; he chose a diversity of techniques when he prayed. Prayer was not a ritual or commandment; this truly was David being himself when he spoke to God.

Being you is always best! I love what David said, "...he most surely did listen, he came on the double when he heard my prayer."

grandparents—take 1

I love my grandparents! They sure do say and do some funny things sometimes, but what a gift they are to us. This quote by Alex Haley is so true: "Nobody can do for little children what grandparents do. Grandparents sort of sprinkle stardust over the lives of little children."[42]

Grandparents are amazing. They love us unconditionally, give great hugs, and usually make great cookies! Things are almost magical when we're with them. At times as we get older, we get busy with school and life and sometimes we forget about them. But always remember, they've been where you are in life and they lived through it! They are great vessels of experience and wisdom—don't ever forget that!

I want to encourage you, take time each week to either visit with or talk to your grandparents. For some of you, your grandparents are no longer here on earth but the coolest thing is they live on through you! You mean the world to them.

PINK PRAYER

Lord,

Thank You for my grandparents. Thank You they love me and support me. Help me not to take them for granted. Help me to be a blessing to them as they've been to me, in Jesus' name. I love You Lord, Amen.

grandparents—take 2

When you think about your grandparents, what is the first thought that comes to mind— old...funny...out of touch? Sometimes we look more at the outside of our grandparents and forget to look at the inside. For a minute forget about the gray hair, forget they don't wear the same kind of clothes you do, and think about all they've been through in life.

When I think of my grandparents, my first thought is love and the next, wisdom. The older genera- tion is so full of wisdom from years of experience in living life. The Scripture says, "Get wisdom-it's worth more than money; choose insight over income every time" (Prov. 16:16 MSG).

Girls, if you have questions about life, there's no one more qualified to answer them than good ole' Grandma or Grandpa! And if your grandpar- ents aren't on this earth anymore, find a friend's and talk with them. They've been where you are in life—problems with boyfriends, parents, school—and their advice is timeless. There may be times when we forget about them or we think they're too "old fashioned" to have answers to our questions. But, if we give them some of our time, sit with them, listen to their stories, and hear what they've learned, we are always going to come out on top.

Always remember God is the ultimate giver of wisdom, but our grandparents sure do come in a close second. Let's pray:

Lord,

I thank You for my grandparents. What an amazing gift they are to me and my family! Thank You for their wisdom and love. I just pray I am able to be a blessing to them and allow them to be a blessing in my life. I pray health and joy over their lives. Thank You for such a great gift, in Jesus' name. Amen.

think pink

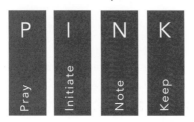

P I N K

Pray Initiate Note Keep

"The wise still seek Him."

—Author Unknown

hang on…help is on the way

My help comes from the LORD, Who made heaven and earth.

Psalm 121:2 NKJV

One of my favorite prayers is just plain, "Help me Lord!" I can't tell you how many times I have made that request even in one day.

One of those times was about five years ago when my youngest son Brock and I were driving back home from Colorado after skiing for a few days. I grew up in Canada and I love the mountains, so every chance I can, I try to spend time there. Anyway, we were about four hours away from home and decided to make one last stop, get a little lunch, and take one last potty break. We pulled into a really nice Subway sandwich shop and Brock got in line while I went to the ladies room. Well, to this day I can hardly believe what happened. I had set my keys and my purse on the back of the tank and as I went to flush the toilet, I hit my big set of keys and they went flyin' right into the swirling flushing water and faster than you could say "NOOOO" they were gone. It wasn't just one key. I had my husband's truck and there were several keys on that ring.

Shortly after I stood there in disbelief, I knew I had to face my son and all the other people out there who I had to tell they couldn't use the bathroom until we had a plumber come out and try to retrieve the keys. That's when I said, "Help me Lord—please help me!" I really didn't know any other prayer to pray for this particular circumstance.

I quietly told my son and he just said, "You what?" but he was actually very sweet about it. Then I whispered to a very kind lady across the counter and she said in quite a loud voice, "You flushed your keys down the toilet!" There were about ten people in line that heard and many of them participated in quite a chuckle. One lady spoke up and said, "By gosh, you'll never get them keys back. The toilets in these new restaurants are way to powerful. Those keys are probably all the way to China by now, Hon'."

An older couple pulled my son and I aside and asked if we believed in God and we said, "Absolutely!" Then they said, "Well we're just going to pray and believe you'll get them back." They knew it was a Saturday and it would cost an arm and a leg for a plumber and locksmith and they wanted to believe with us.

Then this precious young manager came over to us and said, "Why don't you order some lunch. I would like to call my grandpa and have him see if he can get to those keys." I said, "Please don't bother him," but he insisted before we call a plumber to let him give it a shot. In no time this wonderful eighty year old man came shuffling into the restaurant and he, his grandson, Brock, and I were all standing in the bathroom.

The grandson said, "Do you believe in God? My grandpa and I are Christians and we would like to pray." He proceeded to pray, "Lord, please help us get to those keys, in Jesus' name. Amen." We all agreed and within moments that sweet grandpa had that whole toilet pulled off and felt around all those pipes until we heard a little jingle. He grabbed a tool and was able to get a hold of that big wad of keys! Needless to say, we were all laughing and saying, "Thank You Lord." I am a hugger, so I was hugging everyone and thanking them so much for their help.

We would have had to pay a plumber or a locksmith but this way we were able to give the young manager and his grandpa some much deserved cash. They didn't want to take it but we insisted. I thought it was so awesome that we met the kindest people (I'll never forget them) and we were only about an hour behind on our trip.

When we got in the truck to head home, I thanked Brock for being so patient and understanding and for having such a good sense of humor. He replied, "Well Mom, I was being patient on the outside but on the inside I was a little angry." I would never have known.

We got home safe and sound that evening and the next morning I went to get my car keys to head to church. My husband had to leave earlier that morning but found enough time to attach my car keys to a bright orange twelve inch buoy so they would always stay afloat. He thought he was pretty funny. It was really clever, I do have to admit. That following week I made sure to call the main Subway office to tell them about the wonderful young man they had working for their company.

All that to say, "Help me Lord!" is a very good prayer to pray. All through the Bible, great men and woman declare their help has come from the Lord when they asked. What a very simple, sincere, most powerful prayer. Thank you Lord for helping your children when we ask!

Father,

I really need You. I need to know Your love like never before. I don't understand everything that is going on but I also know I don't need to understand it all, as long as I trust You.

You said in Your Word You lift up those who are sad. You are always thinking about me and watching everything that concerns me. I lean on and trust in You completely. Your truth and faithfulness shield me. You are my shepherd and I lack nothing with You. Thank You for restoring my soul. Even as I walk through this valley, I will not fear for You are with me. You comfort me with Your Word and Your Spirit. I choose to completely trust You and I know You're going to help me through this time in my life.

I love You Lord and continue to run to You in good times and bad. Thank You for wrapping Your arms around me and others who are hurting during this time too, in Jesus' name. Amen.

think pink

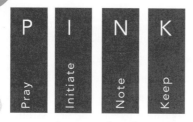

P — Pray
I — Initiate
N — Note
K — Keep

scriptures to trust in

The LORD is my shepherd, I shall not be in want. He makes me lie down in green pastures, he leads me beside quiet waters, he restores my soul. He guides me in paths of righteousness for his name's sake. Even though I walk through the valley of the shadow of death, I will fear no evil, for you are with me; your rod and your staff, they comfort me.

You prepare a table before me in the presence of my enemies. You anoint my head with oil; my cup overflows. Surely goodness and love will follow me all the days of my life, and I will dwell in the house of the LORD forever.

Psalm 23 NIV

As a young girl all I ever thought about was getting married and having babies. I remember the day I finally gave that dream to the Lord, not that it was a wrong desire but I wanted to put God first and trust Him completely with that dream. ("Trust in the LORD with all your heart and lean not on your own understanding. In all your ways acknowledge him and he will make your paths straight.")[43] I felt like God placed that desire in my heart but all I really wanted was to be in His will. He was oh so faithful to see to that.

When I least expected it, a young man who was one of my best friends became my dream come true. I was helping him in a children's ministry team. We would help in our church and travel to different schools and camps. We did a lot of street ministry with puppets and drama, and in the midst of that I found myself falling head over heels for this guy I had known for years.

He had been away at Bible school and came back so changed—so passionate, so kind, such a leader. He was still as fun as I remembered him but so responsible and even though I thought he was "cute" I was drawn to this man of God he had become. What else can I say? One day we were having a puppet practice and he was leading our team in a worship time when all of a sudden, I looked over at him and my heart went pitter patter.

We would always hang out after practice but that day I went straight home to my bedroom, hit my knees, and began a prayer that went something like this: "Father, the devil is a liar and I do not love Blaine Bartel. Please help me understand why I think I'm falling in love with him." You have to understand all the years we were friends, since junior high, he pretty much annoyed, tormented, and teased me. He was a little bit of a smart aleck to say the least and now I was thinking I loved him!

Well, come to find out he was feeling the same way and we've now been married 28 years. I love him even more than ever and I'm so thankful to the Lord for bringing us together. We, to this day, have so much fun. He's a wonderful dad to our three sons and not only is he my best friend, he's my all time favorite pastor and preacher.

My prayer for you, little girlfriend, is that you will trust and hear from God in all your relationships. He will work out every detail in your life and do more than you can ever dare to ask or even dream of (Eph. 3:20).

guy friends

Father,

Thank You for preparing the right young man for my husband. As You do this, I commit to prepare myself to be a godly wife and in the meantime, I ask You for wisdom in choosing my guy friends. Your Word says kindness makes a young man attractive.[44] Thank You for the friendships of kind young men who love the Lord with all of their hearts, souls, minds, and strength and are good to others. I will hear Your voice and I trust You to guide me in my relationships with any young men in my life. I will conduct myself in purity and honor as your daughter, in Jesus' name. Amen.

habits

"Good habits are hard to acquire but easy to live with. Bad habits are easy to acquire but hard to live with."

Anonymous

When I was about ten I was with a group of older girls who I did highland dancing with. We were at a camp and they smoked, so I tried it and unfortunately I liked it. As the years went on I was always sneaking a cigarette here and there. It was easy to do because both my parents smoked and I could just go in the bathroom and hide. That was the part I hated—always hiding.

After I asked Jesus in my heart I had a real hard time giving it up. I hated hiding it from my friends and youth pastors. I would try to quit for awhile, but I just liked it and would start again. I felt so defeated, besides the fact I knew it wasn't healthy, and the whole sneaky business bothered me. The crazy thing is, I know people knew I smoked and you know, they still loved me and probably were praying for me.

From the time I was 10 until I was 18 I smoked. I remember smoking my last few cigarettes on the way to Bible school. It was a four hour drive and I just made a decision from that day on I would never smoke again. I have to tell you, it wasn't easy. I'll never forget one of my prayer times down on my knees beside my bunk bed. I asked the Lord to give me the strength to quit and do you know, He just reminded me of how much He loved me and that He cared about the whole me (my spirit, soul, and body). He showed me that what He did for me on the cross was so I could have power over destructive things like smoking. I just knew I had heard from Him and knew He would help me from then on.

Jesus loved me but when I left that school and went home, back into familiar places, I have to tell you it was tough some days. But I knew in that prayer time Jesus spoke to my heart and gave me the courage to not go backwards.

Please let me say as I share this story, I'm not just singling out smoking. We all have different issues we deal with. It could be addictive habits like eating too many sweets or not eating enough for our bodies to be healthy. Some of us make poor choices for our health. Maybe we shop too much, talk too much, or like me even as a grown woman, I hate to say, I can be pretty disorganized and messy. All these things and more, the Lord cares about and wants to help us if we'll let Him. It's all because He loves us and wants us to benefit and grow in developing good habits.

When we have a taste of victory in our lives it will bring hope—to ourselves and to others. God wants us to be free. It was so important to Him that He gave His only Son to die so we could be free from sin and the negative effects of bad habits. When we realize we're wrong, the first step is to ask Him to forgive us, then let Him help us conquer our bad habits and live our lives in new and healthier ways.

Lord,

I am so thankful You care about everything that concerns me. As You convict me of things that are harmful to me and others, I want to please You. I want to make changes for the better in my life. You have made me new on the inside and I want to clothe myself with Your nature, Your attitudes and thoughts, and be constantly changing for the better. As I read Your Word, pray, and hear Your voice, You give me courage and strength to grow and change. Thank You for loving me and wanting the best for me.

Father, I thank You that the same Spirit that raised Christ from the dead dwells in me and quickens my mortal body.[45] I submit myself to You and resist the devil and what he is trying to do—kill, steal, and destroy me. Thank You Lord for helping me overcome, in Jesus' name.

ask

You can ask for anything in my name, and I will do it, so that the Son can bring glory to the Father. Yes, ask me for anything in my name, and I will do it!

John 14:13-14 NLT

Wow! Is this how you feel when you read this Scripture? Jesus is making it very clear to us in these verses that we can pray (ask) to God, the Father, using His name (in the name of Jesus) and we can ask for anything. He says He will do it. Now be sure to note His words, "for this will bring praise to the Father." I am assuming you are growing and maturing in God's Word daily using this devotional as a guide. So I know that you know "anything" means it would be according to His character and His will. When asking, I encourage you to be sure it would be pleasing to Him. He will never cross His Word or His will for you or for anyone. But the wonderful thing about growing in Him and knowing Him is His will becomes your will.

So begin to pray some big "anything" prayers. He cares about the smallest details of your life (a new pair of jeans for the party), and the biggest things about your life (what college to go to and where to get the finances to pay for it.)

Pray about everything—your family, your friends, your school, your teachers, a job, your actions, your attitude. Pray about anything that concerns you. If it is a concern of yours, it is a concern of Jesus'.

Remember He said, "You can ask for anything in my name and I will do it...Yes, ask anything in my name and I will do it!"

So get busy—start asking.

what's a girl to do?
when her heart is broken

Proverbs 4:23 says that above all else, guard your heart, for it is a wellspring of life. In other words, guarding you heart means to:

Be on the look out
Stay alert
Protect
Shield
Stay on your toes
Be attentive
Keep your eyes peeled and
Keep it under surveillance

You are responsible for this precious heart God gave you. You need to do your part to protect it. Hide God's Word in it. Think about what you're thinking about. Who are you listening to and who are your examples? Ask the Lord to help you with your choices—what you listen to and what you are watching.

However, there may have been times perhaps you didn't see things coming that have really hurt you—times when you have even ended up with a broken heart.

Unfortunately, that has happened to each and every one of us at one time or another but…fortunately, that is exactly why God's son, Jesus, went to the cross. He took upon His own heart every single ounce of rejection, hurt, suffering, pain, agony, grief, and distress that has ever or will ever try to crush our heart.

My dear little girlfriend…let the healing begin. Our heavenly Father is just waiting for our consent to let Him wrap His arms around us so we can receive His healing touch. It's only in His presence we can truly be healed and this is one of the wonderful miracles that begins with our most intimate times with the Lord. He came to heal our broken hearts and that's an absolute promise to you.

Guess what happens as we let the Holy Spirit work in us? We become stronger and stronger and become that girl who helps someone else experience God's healing power.

The broken become masters at mending.

Father,

I come to You in Jesus' name and I give to You my broken heart. I never want to hide anything from You. I trust You to heal me like only You can. Thank You for sending Jesus to heal my broken heart, bind up my wounds, and take all my pain and sorrow.[46] Thank You for sending Your Word to heal me and deliver me from all destruction.[47]

I also want to thank You for Your grace to help me forgive those who have hurt me.[48] I choose to obey You. You have forgiven me of so much and that's why I know with Your help and love, I can forgive.

I praise You for making me whole so I am good and ready to help You mend others whose hearts are broken. I will continue to guard my heart so it can be a wellspring of life.[49]

"The dying Jesus is the evidence of God's anger toward sin; but the living Jesus is the proof of God's love and forgiveness."

—Lorenz Eifert

20th Century Minister

keep lookin' up

When we keep our eyes on Jesus (look up), it's really hard to look down on others. Our lives are filled with relationships and as we set our hearts to love people as God's daughters, He has promised to help us. His grace is amazing! The Bible says that the love of God has been poured into our hearts by the Holy Spirit (Rom. 5:5).

Have you ever been so angry with someone or so annoyed that you don't feel like you even love them? When we get in a spot like that we only have one best choice and that is to look up to Jesus Who is the Word of God. As we turn to His instruction about love and ask Him to help us see people through His eyes and His heart, I assure you that our hearts will want nothing less than God's best for that person. Our heavenly Father is so pleased when we choose to look up to Him. His love never fails.

Let's be the kind of girls that do not give up on anyone just like God doesn't give up on us.

Sometimes a girl who prays is asked to stand in the gap for someone who just doesn't understand God's love—just like Jesus sacrificed Himself so we could receive forgiveness and understand His Father's love. We don't always feel like taking the time to pray for others but when we choose to take a little time, we're sowing good seed and will one day see a person's life restored and made whole. How amazing to be a part of seeing someone's life changed for eternity because we let God's love be in charge of our hearts.

God bless you, God's daughter! Don't get weary in your well doing.

Love,
Cathy

"How sweet the name
of Jesus sounds
In a believer's ear;
It soothes his sorrows,
heals his wounds,
And drives away
his fear."

—John Newton

Author of the hymn,
Amazing Grace

For the LORD grants wisdom! From his mouth come knowledge and understanding.

Proverbs 2:6 NLT

Father,

I could really use some help with my homework and I am asking You to help me and give me wisdom.[50] I know I am to be diligent and to do everything as unto the Lord. Help me have a good attitude. You said in Luke 16:10 (NLT), "If you are faithful in little things, you will be faithful in large ones. But if you are dishonest in little things, you won't be honest with greater responsibilities."

I don't understand why I have to know all of the things I am learning in school but I do realize as I study I am developing good habits for my future. I believe You will help me stay focused and complete the assignments I've been given, in Jesus' name. Amen.

never, never give up

Sometimes when we have been let down over and over again, it's just plain hard to have hope. We can be afraid to put our hope in anyone or anything ever again. Please don't give up. We've got to press on.

The Lord says to us "Don't lose heart...don't lose hope." He does hear us and He does have an answer for us. We can't let go. Whether we are praying for a loved one or need help in our own lives, we must have hope. Hope is the springboard for faith and love. We have God's grace and the knowledge He truly loves us and knowing the truth of His promises will encourage us and help us to persevere.

think pink

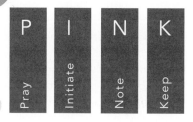

P	I	N	K
Pray	Initiate	Note	Keep

scriptures to press on

For everything that was written in the past was written to teach us, so that through endurance and the encouragement of the Scriptures we might have hope.

Romans 15:4 NIV

May the God of hope fill you with all joy and peace as you trust in him, so that you may overflow with hope by the power of the Holy Spirit.

Romans 15:13 NIV

hope

Not that I have already obtained all this, or have already been made perfect, but I press on to take hold of that for which Christ Jesus took hold of me. Brothers, I do not consider myself yet to have taken hold of it. But one thing I do: Forgetting what is behind and straining toward what is ahead, I press on toward the goal to win the prize for which God has called me heavenward in Christ Jesus.

Philippians 3:12-14 NIV

But the eyes of the LORD are on those who fear him, on those whose hope is in his unfailing love.

Psalm 33:18 NIV

hope

Thank you Father,

For the hope I have in You. I choose to put my hope in Your unfailing love for me.[51] Thank You for helping me to press on toward the goal to win the prize which You have called me to.[52] Thank You for giving me joy and peace as I trust in You so that I will overflow with hope and with the power of the Holy Spirit.[53] I love that You say I can overflow with hope because that means I'll have hope to give to others too, in Jesus' name I pray. Amen.

"It is not the body's posture, but the heart's attitude that counts when we pray."[54]
—Billy Graham

Evangelist

prayer—here, there, and everywhere

One of the most freeing and comforting things I learned as a young Christian girl was I could pray absolutely anywhere. I just knew God would hear me whether I was in my bedroom, on my knees, lying down, drying my hair, putting on my makeup, quietly under my breath at the bus stop, on the school bus, or at my desk at school. As I got older I prayed in the car, at the grocery store, folding the laundry, and also in my favorite chair. I know you get my point.

It's very important to have a time set apart to read our Bible and get alone with God and pray. Some people like to keep a little notebook or prayer journal and write things down—maybe even play some worship music. The main thing is we take time as often as we can to talk to and hear from our heavenly Father. God loves us and will speak to us anywhere and listen to us always.

my future husband:
a prayer of surrender
of your heart

Father,

As I think about the man I will marry, I submit my heart, my will, and my emotions—all that I am to You. I don't desire a partnership that will be merely compatible or "mostly happy." More than happiness, more than any personality traits or characteristics, I desire to be in that one partnership that will bring You the most glory, delight, and satisfaction.

You are my Creator, You knit me together in my mother's womb. My frame was not hidden from you when I was made in that secret place. When I was woven together in the depths of the earth, Your eyes saw my unformed body and all the days ordained for me were written down in Your book before one of them came to be. Not only my

Creator, but the Creator of all things—how amazing You are.[55]

Let me always consider the heart of a man. Let me consider first and foremost what You think— what Your purpose is. Father, I pray my heart won't find rest in a decision unless it's 100% Your choice. I purpose to not be swayed by the outward appearance of a person—the way he looks, the way he dresses. I won't be swayed by romantic words or thoughts. I won't be swayed by butterflies in my stomach. Father, I will only be swayed by Your Word and Your thoughts. When You say "Yes!" I'll delight in everything You created him to be. I will find him the most attractive, inside and out, if You find his heart good, his life pleasing.

Lord, You alone know the end from the beginning. You alone love me like no one else ever could. You are always aware of my need and seek to satisfy my deepest longings. You can see through my temporary wants which have no power to bring joy or fulfillment. How could I trust anyone else but You? I don't trust myself—only You leading me.

Your Word is more valuable to me than the voices of a hundred friends saying, "Yes! He's the one!" Father, until I hear it from You, seal up my affections, let them rest in You alone. Take ownership of them. When the time comes, pour out my affections (as they are a manifestation of Your love) on the right man at the right time. Help me to never think too small or too hastily, in Jesus' name.

All of this I give You in exchange for the adornment of the hidden person of the heart with the incorruptible beauty of a gentle and quiet spirit which is precious in Your sight Father.[56]

missionaries

Father,

Thank You that I get to pray for missionaries around the world. I understand it is a powerful and important part of missions. Thank You that the doors are open wide for Your Word to be spread and that missionaries have favor with government officials, leaders, and everyone they speak with.

Lord, I ask You to prepare hearts to hear the Word, receive it, and become witnesses of Your glory to the ends of the earth. Thank You and praise You in advance for countless salvations and miracles. And Lord, I pray that You would keep each and every missionary and their family protected from harm and in good health. I ask that You would open the hearts of Your people to support them in every area of need—financially, in prayer, and with new laborers to help spread Your Word. Guard their hearts and minds and give them wisdom for every new day, in Jesus name I pray, Amen.

think pink

P	I	N	K
Pray	Initiate	Note	Keep

missions

Has God ever placed a special tug in your heart for missions? I strongly encourage you to pray about taking a mission's trip with your own church or a teen missions' organization one day soon. I know so many young people who have been changed forever by going on a mission's trip, including my three sons. Every one of them would agree that God used them to reach people in ways they never thought possible! I can promise you this, your life will never be the same after a mission's experience.

my nation

Do you sometimes wonder why you have been so blessed to live in this amazing country? Especially when you hear about all the trouble and sorrow that so many others around the world face each day! I know your mom and dad, and probably your youth pastor, have reminded you of this many times over. But if you really pause and consider this, is it not reassuring to you that you were chosen by your Maker and your Father to be blessed. This should be high on your list of "I get to."

Because you live in this great land, you get to pray for this land to remain great and to remain under the guidance of Almighty God. We can be warriors for our country in these unsettling times through prayer. Go for it! Be a *prayer warrior!*

The first thing I want you to do is pray. Pray every way you know how, for everyone you know. Pray especially for rulers and their governments to rule well so we can be quietly about our business of living simply, in humble contemplation. This is the way our Savior God wants us to live.

1 Timothy 2:1-3 MSG

Father,

I get to and want to pray for my nation as You tell me in this Scripture. So I hold up my country, our President and our government and ask You to help them rule righteously so we all can live simply and humbly as You want us to. I agree with Your Word, as my nation serves You, we will live in safety and joy no matter what is happening all around us.

You tell us in spite of trouble, overwhelming victory is ours through Your Son, Jesus the Christ, our Lord and Savior, because He loves us. You also tell us that Your hand holds our President's heart and You lead him in peace because we please You.

I pray Your Word continues to spread around the world and that there are many new believers because the Good News is delivered to them. I pray all this in the name above all names, Jesus!

think pink

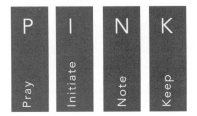

P **Pray**
I **Initiate**
N **Note**
K **Keep**

scriptures for our nation

What joy for the nation whose God is the LORD, whose people he has chosen as his inheritance.

Psalm 33:12 NLT

GOD's a safe-house for the battered, a sanctuary during bad times. The moment you arrive, you relax; you're never sorry you knocked.

Psalm 9:9-10 MSG

No, despite all these things, overwhelming victory is ours through Christ, who loved us.

Romans 8:37 NLT

In the LORD's hand the king's heart is a stream of water that he channels toward all who please him.

Proverbs 21:1 NIV

Meanwhile, the word of God continued to spread, and there were many new believers.

Acts 12:24 NLT

hurts

Dear little sister,

I want to share something on my heart.

You may be struggling with very difficult circumstances in your family. If you're not, please bear with me because I believe what I am saying may help you to help some of your dear friends now or even in the future.

First let me say I am so sorry if you are having to deal with any kind of heartache at all, whether it be divorce, a parent or sibling fighting an addiction, someone in your home suffering with depression, suicidal thoughts—attempts or if you lost someone to suicide, or any kind of abuse. Maybe you have a parent who is dealing with a horrible sickness. You personally may be fighting any one of these battles yourself.

I just want you to know that as I write this, I realize I may never know exactly what you're going through but I do know your heavenly Father does and I want to remind you to set your hope on Him and do not let go. I've lived through some of these very afflictions and wish I could say it wasn't so bad…but that wouldn't be very honest of me. I want acknowledge right now if you are living in any of these circumstances I know it's not one bit fun and not at all easy.

I grew up in a home with an alcoholic mom. Let me say I share this story with so much honor, love, and respect for my dad and mom; my mom told me several years ago that I could tell anyone about her life if it would help them. She and my dad have been in heaven for several years now and oh, how I miss them, but I have to admit there were times as a young girl and young woman that they made me so angry.

I was twenty years old when they got divorced and even as a grown up young married woman it felt like someone took a pair of scissors and cut me right down the middle. So if you've been through that or are in the midst of it, I can relate to you. I finally had to come to an understanding my parents were hurting just as much or even more than my younger brother, sister, and me. These are the times, as hard as they are, we need to surrender our broken hearts to Jesus and let Him do His work on us and our family. We have to keep our hearts tender and in an attitude of forgiveness for God to help us to get back up and go on.

I really can't ever remember as a little girl my mom not having a drinking problem. I started to figure it out when I was about seven or eight years old. As a teenager, it just got worse and worse with several suicide attempts and many weeks at a time in hospitals and rehab facilities. I think the part that made it so hard was I knew what good, loving, giving, kind, and caring people my parents were. But they were also broken and hurting and as a kid I just didn't know how to help.

When I was about thirteen, I asked Jesus into my heart because of a precious great aunt and uncle who gave my dad and mom a Bible. I took it in my room one night and in it was a prayer that I prayed and I knew something happened in my heart. I'd never be the same again and though our circumstances didn't change for years, I was able to see my parents through God's eyes. I still got angry at times and said the wrong thing way too often but I would ask the Lord and my parents to forgive me. I was determined to never let go of them in prayer.

Prayer was without a doubt the one constant in my life that helped me the most. Knowing the Lord heard my prayers brought more comfort to me than anyone will ever know. I was always so afraid for my mom's life. She was so hard on herself. I never knew if she was going to be there when I came home from school or what kind of shape my little brother, sister, and I would find her in.

As I share this, I am thinking of you. Not knowing exactly what you are going through or what you have been through, I want you to be aware that there is help for you. I was so fortunate to know my dad and mom had friends and family who were always trying to help. When I asked Jesus into my heart, I was able to turn to my youth pastors and others in my church, especially women who would pray with me for my family.

I really want to emphasize right now that if you or any member of your family is in danger because of abuse (physical, emotional, sexual), addictions, depression, thoughts of suicide, or anything detrimental, please ask for help. There are people who can help you take steps to restore yourself and your family. Please find someone you can trust—maybe a pastor, someone at school, or look in the phone book or online for a teen hotline. You may have a friend whose mom you can talk to.

Whether it is you or a family member struggling with any of these destructive behaviors, I want you to know God loves you and your family too much to let your life continue in such harm—you have got to get help. The longer we keep hurtful things hidden, the more damage can be done. Please don't isolate yourself. I totally understand...sometimes we feel like nobody will get it but know this, God loves you and there are truly good people who do get it, can help you, and want to be there for you. Put your trust in God to show you who and know we really do need one another. The worst thing you can do is pull away from everyone. If it's you struggling with an addiction, depression, any kind of emotional pain, abuse, maybe you're pregnant, you may have had an abortion...I can't say it enough: *Please* tell someone who can help you.

Maybe you think you've gone too far and no one will ever forgive you. That is a big fat lie from hell. Even if you think you've disappointed everyone and their opinion of you has changed, well let me tell you something: you are so valuable to God. He gave His most beloved Son for you. You, my dear girl, were bought with a great price. Jesus gave His life so that you can live, not so bad people would be good but so hurting, broken people could be healed and made whole—to live a life of joy, know real love, and give love to others. So don't you ever give up on yourself, your loved ones, or your friends. Always remember too, if you have a friend going through these kinds of battles, be a true friend and help them get help. They may need you to gently guide them in the right direction.

When we speak of these issues, we can't take them lightly. There are times in all of our lives that we just need someone to stand with us, help us see clearly, and be truthful with us. There is no shame in getting help in any area of our lives.

Some of the things we have just talked about are very serious issues and I can't stress enough for you to ask for help whether for yourself or on behalf of your family or friends. They may even be angry but it's worth it to begin a work of healing in their lives. The Lord will give you wisdom if you just ask Him.

Also remember to be patient with yourself, others, and with God. Healing is a process and as we let God work in us and through us, step by step, we will see change in ourselves and those around us. This is a time to hold on like never before to the promises of God and remember no matter what you are feeling, God loves you...He loves you...and He loves all of you. That is the truth and you need to know above all else, nothing can separate you from the love of God.

My prayer is that as you read this, God's love is touching you and your family and you are strengthened and encouraged to press on and *never let go.* God love you and bless you in every part of your heart and life.

If you are struggling in any area and need to talk with someone, please refer to the resources I've listed at the back of the book.

With Love,
Cathy

for my parents

Father,

I just want to say thank You for my parents. I am a disciple taught by You Lord and I desire to honor my dad and mom as Your Word teaches me.[58] I know that no one is perfect so please help me to be patient with my parents and help them to be patient and understanding with me too. Help them to train me up in the way I should go.[59] Thank You for Your love You have poured into all of our hearts by Your Holy Spirit.[60]

Give me ideas to help my mom and dad around our house; I know how much they do and how much they work to provide for our family. I just want Your grace and peace to be multiplied to them.[61] Help us to communicate and to encourage one another. Thank You for laughter in our home. In good times and difficult times help us to always turn to You Lord. I say Jesus is Lord over our family and my parents have wisdom to train and discipline me as You would have them to in Jesus' name I pray. Amen.

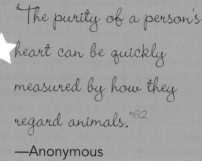

"The purity of a person's heart can be quickly measured by how they regard animals."[62]

—Anonymous

"Animals are such agreeable friends—they ask no questions, they pass no criticisms."[63]

—George Eliot
17th Century English Novelist

my pet(s)

i love my pet(s)

Pets can be such wonderful friends and an important part of our life, bringing lots of laughter and joy. Do you have a pet that you consider to be a best friend? Maybe it's a dog, cat, or even a fish? God created such a variety of animals, with dogs alone there are over 400 reported breeds in the entire world! I wonder if they have a mix between a Chihuahua and a Great Dane.

I've had several pets, mostly dogs, throughout my life. They may be a lot of work at times, with all of the accidents, eating things they shouldn't, or having to give them baths, but without a doubt they are some of the best little God-given friends to our family. I love how pets can be there for you in ways that sometimes other friends are not. If treated well and shown a little love and attention, pets give us their unconditional love and companionship in return. They desperately want our friendship and express overwhelming joy when it's given…imagine if people acted like that! Plus, they are the best at keeping secrets and snuggling up when you feel sad or lonely.

Next time you look at your pet think of how God has blessed you with a friend like no other and thank Him for the opportunity to care for one of His unique little creations!

think pink

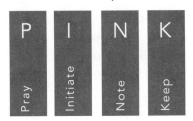

P — Pray
I — Initiate
N — Note
K — Keep

the bed puppy

Now I lay me down to sleep,
My giant bed is soft and deep.
I sleep right in the center groove
My human friend can hardly move!

I've trapped her legs, she's tucked in tight
And here is where I spend the night
No one disturbs me or dares intrude
Till morning comes and "I want food!"

So thank you Lord for giving me
This human friend that I see.
The one who hugs and holds me tight
And shares her bed with me at night![64]

Ellen Morris

my pet(s)

Father,

Thank You for my pet(s), _____. Thank You for showing me love through them and for even using them to show me how to be a better friend. Help my pet(s) to be obedient and help me to understand how to train them. Please keep them safe and protected from harm, giving them a long and healthy life. I promise to love and take care of the little friend(s) You've given to me, in Jesus name. Amen.

Father,

Thank You that I am your child. Your Word says that when I resist the devil, he flees from me.[65] I declare no weapon formed against me shall prosper.[66]

Today, I put on the whole armor of God: my waist is wrapped with truth, I wear the breastplate of righteousness, my feet are prepared to proclaim the gospel of peace, and I take the shield of faith, which quenches all the fiery darts of the wicked. This is all possible because I wear the helmet of salvation and wield the sword of the Spirit, which is the word of God.[67]

I walk in Your protection because I am praying always with all prayer and supplication in the Spirit, and watching with all perseverance and supplication for all saints.[68] I take authority over this day and believe it will be prosperous for me.

I am the righteousness of God in Christ Jesus.[69] I belong to God and I am His property. Satan, you are bound from my family, my mind, my body, my home, and my finances.[70] I am healed by the stripes of Jesus.[71] Whatsoever I set my hands to do shall prosper for God supplies all my needs.[72]

God, I pray for the ministry You have set before me. Anoint me Lord for all You have called me to do. You are going before me to set divine appointments and open doors of opportunities.

I have a hedge of protection, because of the powerful blood of Jesus, around myself and my loved ones day and night.[73] I ask you Father, in the name of Jesus, to surround us with Your angels today and everyday.[74] I call on Your holy angels to protect my house from any intrusion and to protect me and my family.

I am reminded of Psalm 91 (NLT) and believe it:

> "Those who live in the shelter of the Most High will find rest in the shadow of the Almighty. This I declare about the LORD: He alone is my refuge, my place of safety; he is my God, and I trust him. For he will rescue you from every trap and protect you from deadly disease. He will cover you with his feathers. He will shelter you with his wings. His faithful

promises are your armor and protection. Do not be afraid of the terrors of the night, nor the arrow that flies in the day. Do not dread the disease that stalks in darkness, nor the disaster that strikes at midday. Though a thousand fall at your side, though ten thousand are dying around you, these evils will not touch you. Just open your eyes, and see how the wicked are punished. If you make the LORD your refuge, if you make the Most High your shelter, no evil will conquer you; no plague will come near your home. For he will order his angels to protect you wherever you go. They will hold you up with their hands so you won't even hurt your foot on a stone. You will trample upon lions and cobras; you will crush fierce lions and serpents under your feet! The LORD says, 'I will rescue those who love me. I will protect those who trust in my name. When they call on me, I will answer; I will be with them in trouble. I will rescue and honor them. I will reward them with a long life and give them my salvation.'"

I ask all of this in the name of Jesus. Amen.

understanding

The eyes of your understanding being enlightened; that ye may know what is the hope of his calling, and what the riches of the glory of his inheritance in the saints.

Ephesians 1:18

How many times have you said, "I don't understand the Bible?" You can and you will if you take the time to pray this Scripture. As a young woman of God, ask your heavenly Father to give you spiritual understanding as you study His Word. He can help you understand and apply it to your life.

The *Amplified Bible* puts it this way: "By having the eyes of your heart flooded with light, so that you can know and understand the hope to which He has called you, and how rich is His glorious inheritance in the saints (His set-apart ones)." You will be amazed how understanding will begin to come as you spend time in His Word each day. Your Father gave you His Word to guide you and lead you in your daily life. He never intended it to be hard to understand. However, the Bible is a spiritual book; so you must approach it in a spiritual way—through prayer. You have His Holy Spirit living in you if you have accepted Christ. You are a spiritual being.

Whenever you pick up your Bible, pray this prayer. It works!

Father,

Thank You that as I read Your Word today, You flood the eyes of my heart with Your light, so that I can know and understand the hope to which You have called me, and how rich is Your glorious inheritance in me. I have been set-apart to serve You, in Jesus' name.

The Lord is waiting for you to call out to Him today so He can answer you. Remember, He is your Father God!

think pink

P — Pray
I — Initiate
N — Note
K — Keep

prevailing prayer

At the close of a prayer-meeting, the pastor observed a little girl, about twelve years of age, remaining upon her knees, when most of the congregation had retired. Thinking the child had fallen asleep, he touched her, and told her it was time to return home. To his surprise, he found that she was engaged in prayer, and he said: "All things, whatsoever ye ask in prayer, believing, ye shall receive."[75] She looked at her pastor earnestly, and inquired: "Is it so? Does God say that?" He took up a Bible, and read the passage aloud. She immediately commenced praying: "Lord, send my Father here; Lord, send my father to the church."

Thus she continued for about half an hour, attracting by her earnest cry the attention of persons who lingered about the door. At last a man rushed into the church, ran up the aisle, and sank upon his knees by the side of his child, exclaiming: "What do you want of me?" She threw her arms about his neck, and began to pray: "O Lord, convert my father!" Soon the man's heart was melted, and he began to pray for himself.

The child's father was three miles from the church when she began praying for him. He was packing goods in a wagon, and felt impressed with an irresistible impulse to return to his house. He left the goods in the wagon, and hastened to the church, where he found his daughter crying mightily to God in his behalf; and he was there led to the Savior.

Foster's Cyclopedia

save my family

He then brought them out and asked, "Sirs, what must I do to be saved?" They replied, "Believe in the Lord Jesus, and you will be saved—you and your household."

Acts 16:30-31 NIV

He said to his disciples, "The harvest is great, but the workers are few. So pray to the Lord who is in charge of the harvest; ask him to send more workers into his fields."

Matthew 9:37-38 NLT

Lord Jesus,

I believe You when You promise to save both me and my family. Thank You for my salvation and as your daughter, I trust You with my family and I love that You and I are working together to help them to receive the fullness of Your salvation. My heart is set to obey You and do whatever it takes to show them Your love. Even as I am praying right now I believe You are working in their hearts.

Father, You said You are the Lord of the harvest and if I would pray, that You would send more laborers into the fields. So Father I do ask You to send Your workers into my family's lives. Thank You for loving my family and rescuing them from darkness into light. I want them to know You and Your ways and plans for them.

I make myself available to be that laborer to someone else's family. I want to know when I get to heaven I've been obedient and been an answer to someone's prayer in telling their family You love them and in showing them Your goodness.

I praise You and thank You for my family and that I can be an influence for You to them. Show me what to do in Jesus' name.

think pink

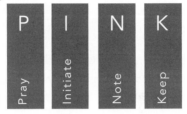

P **Pray**
I **Initiate**
N **Note**
K **Keep**

Jesus knows

JESUS UNDERSTANDS EVERYTHING
WE ARE GOING THROUGH.

We have a great high priest. He has gone up into the heavens. He is Jesus the Son of God. So let us hold firmly to what we say we believe. We have a high priest who can feel it when we are weak and hurting. We have a high priest who has been tempted in every way, just as we are. But he did not sin. So let us boldly approach the throne of grace. Then we will receive mercy. We will find grace to help us when we need it.

Hebrews 4:14-16 NIRV

Thank You, Father,

For my teachers, principals, coaches, all the maintenance men and women, the cafeteria staff, and all the other people who work and volunteer at my school. Thank You for their kind hearts and that they care about young people. Please help me to be an example in my school to respect all of these people as authorities in my life. I commit to pray for them and to always be mindful to thank them for all they do to keep our school running.

I realize there are probably days they would rather be doing something else, so I ask You to use me and others to encourage them and if they don't know You that You Father, the Lord of the harvest, would send laborers into their path to bring Your love and good news to them.[76]

Father, thank You for touching all of the school staff with Your strength and joy to carry on and continue to help them be patient with all of us kids, in Jesus name. God bless my school!

think pink

pink lipstick

According to a news report, a certain private school in Washington was recently faced with a unique problem. A number of 12 year old girls had begun to use lipstick and would put it on in the bathroom.

That was fine, but after they put on their lipstick they would press their lips to the mirror leaving dozens of little lip prints. Every night the maintenance man would remove them and the next day the girls would put them back.

Finally the principal decided that something had to be done. She called all the girls to the bathroom and met them there with the maintenance man. She explained that all these lip prints were causing a major problem for the custodian who had to clean the mirrors every night (you can just imagine the yawns from the little princesses).

To demonstrate how difficult it was to clean the mirrors, she asked the maintenance man to show the girls how much effort was required. He took out a long-handled squeegee, dipped it in the toilet, and cleaned the mirror with it. Since then, there have been no lip prints on the mirror.

There are teachers…and then there are educators.

serving is cool

If any of you wants to serve me, then follow me. Then you'll be where I am, ready to serve at a moment's notice. The Father will honor and reward anyone who serves me.

John 12:26 msg

It's pretty wonderful that as we serve Jesus, the Father will honor us. There are so many ways to serve others. Just look around. We can help out at home and if you don't already do, it would be fun just to see how you can shock your family.

How about at church? You have so much to give whether it's in the nursery, greeting, or helping your youth pastor and his wife. I remember one of my youth pastors wasn't married and really needed help from some of the girls to pray with other girls, to pick up little girls that needed rides to some activities, even to bring food or decorate the youth room for different things. My best friend and I got to help with a lot of these things and we learned so much.

Looking back we can both say, not knowing at the time we would both marry pastors, how grateful we are for some very good training. We were learning to be bold and pray for young women and just learning to be ready to serve.

I'm so thankful for the wonderful people in our church who serve and touch people's lives week in and week out. We have such wonderful young women just like you helping in our children's classes who may never hear of a young mom and dad whose marriage was saved because they got to sit in a service and hear a life changing message while their kids were having a blast and being ministered to. You are not too young to be involved. Pray and ask the Lord to show you what to do. Let's serve the Lord with gladness and watch your Father honor you and even use you to be someone's answer to a prayer.

Some of the definitions of *serve* are "to render assistance, be of use, help," or "to be in the service of."[77] Remember, you are never too young to serve. When you are serving someone, you are giving a part of yourself to them. Jesus stated in Matt 20:28 (NLT), "For even the Son of Man came not to be served but to serve others and to give his life as a ransom for many." Jesus came to earth to serve us. Can you believe that? What a backward thought. The Almighty, the Son of God, our Savior came to earth to serve us. He set the ultimate example.

Just as Jesus served us, we're here to serve others. Here are three places you can serve and show Christ in your everyday life:

School: What a great opportunity to witness to others. Let someone go before you in line at lunch, help a friend in need, or sit with someone who needs a friend.

Home: You can clean up in the kitchen after dinner without being asked or bake cookies for everyone. There are so many things to choose from!

Church: Whether you're gifted in singing, meeting new people, or working with babies, you're giving a part of you to help someone else.

> If anyone serves, he should do it with the strength God provides, so that in all things God may be praised through Jesus Christ.
>
> 1 Peter 4:11 NIV

PINK PRAYER

serving with joy

Lord,

Please show me what I can do to serve and bring honor to You. Thank You for giving me the strength and joy I need in order to lift You higher in my life.[78] I am good to go and want to be like You in serving people. I pray for situations to arise where I will be able to serve whether in my family, my church, my school, my work, or my neighborhood. Help me to lighten the load for someone everyday. I put You first and dedicate my life to serve others just as You came to serve me.[79] I will follow your example, in Jesus' name. Amen.

hospitality

Do not forget or neglect or refuse to extend hospitality to strangers [in the brotherhood (*or* *sisterhood*)—being friendly, cordial, and gracious, sharing the comforts of your home and doing your part generously], for through it some have entertained angels without knowing it.

Hebrews 13:2 AMP

"Hospitality" is derived obviously from the word *hospital*. Webster's defines hospital, "where the sick or injured are given medical care."[57] The above Scripture is applicable to all persons in the body of Christ, including you as a young woman of God. There could be friends at school, in your neighborhood, or at church who are emotionally and spiritually wounded—who are lonely, or who feel like they have no one who will listen and talk to them. Your question might be, "What can I do about that?" You may not be equipped to bring counsel to them about their problems; however, the Lord Jesus has equipped you to be a friend, a listener, and an encourager. This is "hospitality" for you amongst your peers.

Ask a girlfriend home for dinner with your family, or suggest she go for a hamburger with you and other friends after school. Look for opportunities where you can be a listener and encourager to a friend in need. I guarantee you will have some words of kindness and strength to offer. Sometimes a friend just needs to laugh and realize life is not as bad as they thought. Invite that girlfriend home to listen to your favorite Christian CD's, get your Bibles out and share some Scriptures that are encouraging to both of you.

It is such a great experience when we are used of the Lord to bring some comfort to a friend. You never know—you may have just made a new "best friend!"

Girlfriend, hospitality has so many aspects. Ask the Lord to give you some great ideas to flow in this gift. Use the sensitivity the Lord Jesus has given you. I think you'll be surprised how easy it is. You never know (as the Scripture says) when you might be entertaining an "angel."

you belong

Every one of us has a longing to be accepted. One of the most important things to remember is how valuable you are to Jesus. He will never leave you.[80] True acceptance begins with knowing who we belong to. When we *know* we are so loved by God, then we start understanding *who we are*. We have the wonderful assurance no matter what people think of us, we don't have to give into peer pressure and make wrong choices to "belong."

The other side of this is when we receive a real understanding of how much God loves us, we will accept people others won't. That's what Jesus did. These people are in our families, our churches, our schools. You name the place and you'll find people who want to belong. As Christians we need to open our hearts and avail ourselves to pray and not be afraid to ask God to give us ideas to reach out.

Remember God is love and when you take that step to love others, He will cause His love in you to grow and grow. God has a rule and it's golden: When we have our heart set on looking out for others, others will reach out to us. God's daughters are good to people and while we're about the business of making others feel accepted, guess what happens? Yep—we will be encouraged and so fulfilled.

share Christ's love

Father,

The bottom line is You love me and You will never leave me alone. As I spend time with You and talk to You throughout the day, speak to me and help me see opportunities to give Your love and encouragement to people in my life. I want to share Your love by accepting people who are crying out for someone to love them. I'm not too young to see people through Your eyes and take steps to help them.

You have called me Your daughter and I trust You to bring people into my life who love me and accept me for who I am. I refuse to compromise what You have taught me about being accepted and I also refuse to be fearful to reach out to those You put in my heart. Thank You Father, for loving me and trusting me to bring Your love and acceptance to others. I love being your messenger in Jesus' precious name. Amen.

something different

Do you ever feel like there is something missing when it comes to your relationship with God? You read your Bible and go to church but deep down you know there is much more. You've known some Christians who just seem so excited about their faith—there is something different about them, but what?

When you make a decision to follow Christ and to make Him your Lord, His life comes into you. That is absolutely the most important and exciting thing that could happen to any human being! But in His Word, God does tell us about something else He wants to do in us and for us. He not only offers us eternal life but He also wants us to be filled with His Spirit.[81]

What does that mean? Looking at examples from the Bible is the best way to understand it (look up some of the Scriptures on pg. 197). Basically, people were becoming Christians and then they found out there was something called "receiving the Holy Spirit." When they asked God to fill them with the Holy Spirit, they began to "speak in tongues."[82] This experience gave them strength and power they needed for their own lives and to tell other people about Jesus.

You might be a Christian today but not filled with the Holy Spirit. Being filled with the Holy Spirit is God's gift to help you on this earth—it will make such a difference in your life every day. You will feel His presence and power in a new way. Speaking in tongues will help you to be strong and resist temptation. It will allow you to pray about things you don't understand or know with your mind (like your future or praying for others).[83]

The Bible talks about being hungry for God. You know when you are hungry you can't think about anything else (all you want is to dig into that candy bar!) If you truly desire to connect with God—then push everything else aside and take some time to get alone with Him. Put on some worship music. Sing out loud and talk to God from your heart. Ask Him to fill you with His Spirit. Then open up your mouth and let your spirit lead your mind and your tongue. Move your mouth and let God say something through you. It will be with words you don't understand (that is what people call "speaking in tongues"). Without a doubt you will feel closer to God than ever and you will never be the same. Don't let it be just a one-time experience. Let your spirit connect with His Spirit every day.

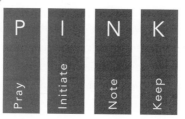

think pink

P I N K

Pray · Initiate · Note · Keep

scriptures on praying in the Spirit

1. Mark 16:15-17 (Jesus' last words on this earth to us.)

2. Acts 8:14-17 (examples of how christians got filled with the spirit.)

3. Acts 10:45-46

4. Acts 19:1-6

5. 1 Corinthians 14:4 (speaking in tongues builds up your spirit.)

6. Romans 8:26-28

7. Jude 20

valuable

Do you want to know what you have in common with all the diamonds and jewels, gold and silver? Let's just say how valuable you are and what a treasure you are—*you* are one of a kind, a masterpiece. You've been bought with a great price.

What if we think in terms of "less is more" when we spend time on our outter beauty, and "more is more" when it comes to spending time on our inner beauty. I'm not saying not to spend time on our outward appearance. The Lord wants us to have fun with makeup, hair, jewelry, our wardrobe, and to absolutely take care of our bodies but remember what we let God do in our hearts is going to sparkle far beyond any trend or fashion. No makeup or outfit will ever give us the power to be transformed like time with Jesus.

Never underestimate what He can do in just one heartbeat when you call on His name. You are so loved and so precious to Him. This is my prayer and His plan for you:

The Lord bless you and watch, guard, and keep you; The Lord make His face to shine upon and enlighten you and be gracious (kind, merciful, and giving favor) to you; The Lord lift up His [approving] countenance upon you and give you peace (tranquility of heart and life continually).

Numbers 6:24-26 AMP

shimmer and shine

I will carry myself as an ambassador for God my Father. I will represent with honor the Father, His Son Jesus, and the Holy Spirit.

We represent the King of kings. We have the opportunity to touch the people around us and change the world for good. Our life is not just about us. Our choices affect a lot of people.

Let me be very serious with you for a moment. The choices we make today will most definitely make an impact on our future relationships. I'm talking about your husband and even your sons and daughters—even grandchildren. I know you're probably thinking: *That is so much responsibility!* Yes it is! Being an ambassador for Christ carries great responsibility!

Remember the movie *Princess Diaries* when Mia Thermopolis, an ordinary everyday school girl finds out she is a princess. Her Grandmother tells her she can opt out of her claim to the throne, and at one point she does get really fearful about taking on such a huge task. But in the end she reads a letter from her father that helps her to not be afraid anymore. She gets her eyes off herself and her heart chooses to serve the people of her country. She realizes the people are far more important than her fears. Her father was able to give her courage through the words in a letter he had written for her 16th birthday. He had already passed away so this letter meant so much to her.

Just think about the book full of love letters our heavenly Father has left for us—words of love, courage, hope, words of comfort, wisdom, instruction, and even some correction. Let's live our lives to bring glory to God, knowing whatever He asks us to do, we can do because He will help us. A young woman who lives to please God and lays her life down has chosen to impact others for eternity.

think pink

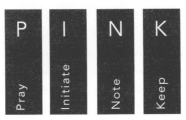

help me shine

God has given me gifts,
God has given me talents.

Please help me Father to be
Disciplined and diligent in
My academics, athletics, or dance
My music or drama

To be a good driver
To pass the test
To share my faith.

Help me to shine in
The way I dress,
The way I wear my make-up,
The way I take care of my body.

Help me to be pure in
My spirit,
My soul,
My body.

Help me to please You
With my thoughts,
With my words,
With my actions.
Amen.

shine on

Father,

Help me to be a light in the darkness to bring hope to hurting and broken people. Help me to bring Your beauty for ashes, the oil of joy for mourning, and the garment of praise for the spirit of heaviness.[84] *I want to radiate Your Spirit—Your love, joy, peace, kindness, patience, goodness, meekness, faithfulness, and self control—so people will see You and give You praise.*[85] *Your light dispels all darkness and all fear. Thank You for Your peace, Your joy, and Your love shining on to others through me, in Jesus' name. Amen.*

checkup

My son, pay attention to what I say; listen closely to my words. Do not let them out of your sight, keep them within your heart; for they are life to those who find them and health to a man's whole body.

Proverbs 4:20–22 NIV

As I was reading this passage and the verses that follow (vv. 20–27) God reminded me His Word is the best place for a little "checkup." So let's walk through the verses for a checkup on ourselves:

 Ears—incline your ear to my sayings (v.20).

 Heart—watch over your heart with all diligence (v.23).

 Mouth—put away a deceitful mouth and devious lips (v.24).

 Eyes—let your eyes look directly ahead, straight on the path of wisdom (v.25).

5. Feet—watch the path of your feet, turn your foot from evil (v.26,27).

Receiving wisdom will affect our whole person— spirit, soul, and body—all aspects of our life!

for my siblings

Father God,

Thank you for my brother/sister, no matter how I feel about them right now. Forgive me for being caught up in myself some times. Help me to have the discipline and the desire to be a blessing to them.

Thank You that I can pray and make a difference in their life. Your Word says my sincere, heartfelt prayers make tremendous power available (James 5:16). Thank You that power is being released right now as I pray.

Lord, I pray that my brother/sister would love You with all their heart and follow You all their life. Let them see clearly the traps Satan might use to trip them up. Give them strength today to resist temptation.

Thank You for the awesome plan You have for their life.[86]

Help them to grasp how much You love them. As I read Your Words today, strengthen me to walk toward my brother/sister in love and according to Your perfect will.

think pink

scriptures to walk in love

...be gentle, kind, humble, meek, and patient. Put up with each other, and forgive anyone who does you wrong, just as Christ has forgiven you. Love is more important than anything else. It is what ties everything completely together. Each one of you is part of the body of Christ, and you were chosen to live together in peace. So let the peace that comes from Christ control your thoughts. And be grateful. Let the message about Christ completely fill your lives, while you use all your wisdom to teach and instruct each other. With thankful hearts, sing psalms, hymns, and spiritual songs to God. Whatever you say or do should be done in the name of the Lord Jesus, as you give thanks to God the Father because of him.

Colossians 3:12-17 CEV

what's a girl to do?
when she needs strength

Do you not know?
Have you not heard?
The LORD is the everlasting God,
the Creator of the ends of the earth.
He will not grow tired or weary,
and his understanding no one
can fathom.

He gives strength to the weary
and increases the power of the weak.

Even youths grow tired and weary,
and young men stumble and fall;
but those who hope in the LORD
will renew their strength.

They will soar on wings like eagles;
they will run and not grow weary,
they will walk and not be faint.

Isaiah 40:28-31 NIV

strength

Father,

You don't faint or grow weary but instead You give power and strength to the faint and weary. You even cause it to multiply and abound. I'm so thankful I'm Your daughter.

Your Word says even young people can stumble and feel exhausted and I want you to know that's where I'm at. Thank You for letting me know if I expect, look for, and put my hope in You that You will change and renew my strength and power. I will lift up my wings and mount up close to You, like an eagle. You will help me run and not be weary and when I walk, I won't faint or become tired. Oh, how I need Your strength and right now I receive this promise in my heart. I ask You to teach me how to wait on You and I pray this in the name of Your Son, Jesus.[87]

to pray or not to pray

Then he returned and found the disciples asleep. He said to Peter, "Simon, are you asleep? Couldn't you watch with me even one hour? Keep watch and pray, so that you will not give in to temptation. For the spirit is willing, but the body is weak."

Mark 14:37-38 NLT

Do you dread tests like I do? It is not so much the test I don't look forward to, but the time leading up to it. The choices we make will determine the outcome. Those who take time and prepare will do well, those who cram usually squeak by, and those who fall asleep...well, let's just say the results show. The same is true with prayer. When we read the chapter the verses above are contained in, we learn the devil tempted both Jesus and the disciples. How they handled the temptation was determined by the choice they had made to pray or not to pray.

Jesus was struggling with the decision to die on the cross for our sins. He decided He would take a few of His disciples to go and pray about the choice He was about to make. Jesus asked some hard questions of the Father during His time in prayer. Everything within Him was saying there had to be another way. Satan also wanted Jesus to go against the plan His Father had, but we see God's Spirit was stronger than how Jesus' body and mind were feeling. Because of His prayer, Jesus overcame temptation and conquered the plan of the enemy.

The disciples, however, chose to give in to temptation. They lost their focus of why Jesus had brought them there. Instead of staying alert and praying for Jesus, they caved into how tired they felt and drifted to sleep. They had no idea their choice to neglect prayer would cause them to fall into more temptation in the hours and days to come.

While the disciples made the wrong choice, we find these young men, most of them teenagers, learned from their mistake and became people of prayer. After Jesus died, rose again, and ascended to heaven we see a radical change in the disciple's prayer life. Their decision to pray changed the world and the church today.[27]

When you accept Christ as your Lord, the Spirit of God comes to live in you.[28] He is stronger than how you feel and any temptation the devil will put in front of you. I believe as God does, as you chose to pray, Satan will leave and your prayers will avail more than you can imagine.

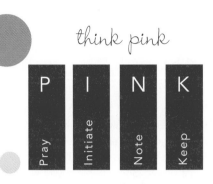

think pink

P — Pray
I — Initiate
N — Note
K — Keep

ups and downs

I love to read through the book of Proverbs. It is so full of simple, yet profound guidance for our lives.

Solomon, who wrote this book for those who were younger in age and faith, was an interesting character. He had an abundance of God's wisdom and yet we see a man who had his own flaws. Reading through another book he wrote, Ecclesiastes, we discover his journey with God was one with many ups and downs. That should encourage all of us. God isn't looking for perfection—only Jesus was perfect. But He is looking for a perfect heart—the kind of heart that always turns back to God when we stumble and fall.

what's a girl to do?
when it's test time

Don't worry about anything, but pray about everything. With thankful hearts offer up your prayers and requests to God. Then, because you belong to Christ Jesus, God will bless you with peace that no one can completely understand. And this peace will control the way you think and feel.

Philippians 4:6-7 CEV

When it comes time for a big test in a class or finals at the end of the year, what is one word that describes most people around you? Stressed! Either that or there are those people who seem to not care at all. So how do you care and yet not get anxious or worried?

Isn't it great when the first school bell rings in the morning, Jesus doesn't say, "Well, I'm outta here—I'm going to go do something more interesting and I'll see you at youth group tonight." No, the Bible says He never leaves us.[88] But the Bible also tells us to stir up the gift of God that is in us.[89] That means even though He is there, we need to invite Him into whatever we are doing.

Wouldn't it be great if we could just shift over to God's Spirit living in us and let Him take the math test? Of course it doesn't work that way (even Jesus had to study when He was on the earth!) but He can work through your mind if you yield to Him. If you feel full of worry, discouragement, and hopelessness before a test, then you are not yielding to God (that is the way Satan wants you to feel). God will always give you a sense of peace and courage. What an awesome advantage we have to be able to ask the Creator of the universe for His guidance!

Do your part by being well prepared for tests. Then ask for His help—to think clearly and to be full of peace. It is okay to feel a little nervous before a test, just like athletes feel a little adrenalin before a race. Just make sure that energy is directed in prayer to God. Write the Scripture from the previous page down on one of your school notebooks and say it to yourself if you start to get worried.

Father God,

Thank You that You are in me and around me as I take this test. You never leave me or forsake me.[90] I command my body to be calm in the name of Jesus and I pray that you help me to recall everything I have studied. My mind is strong, I am encouraged and full of peace. Amen.

think pink

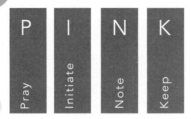

P	I	N	K
Pray	Initiate	Note	Keep

God's answers

YOU SAY	**GOD SAYS**	**BIBLE VERSES**
It's impossible	All things are possible	Luke 18:27
I'm too tired	I will give you rest	Matthew 11:28-30
Nobody really loves me	I love you	John 3:16
I can't go on	My grace is sufficient	2 Corinthians 12:9; Psalm 91:15
I can't figure things out	I will direct your steps	Proverbs 3:5,6
I can't do it	You can do all things	Philippians 4:13
I'm not able	I am able	2 Corinthians 9:8
It's not worth it	It will be worth it	Romans 8:28
I can't forgive myself	I forgive you	1 John 1:9; Romans 8:1
I can't manage	I will supply all your needs	Philippians 4:19
I'm afraid	I have not given you a spirit of fear	2 Timothy 1:7
I'm always worried and frustrated	Cast all your cares on ME	1 Peter 5:7
I'm not smart enough	I give you wisdom	1 Corinthians 1:30
I feel all alone	I will never leave you or forsake you	Hebrews 13:5

watching what I say

Dear God,

You said in the Bible that if I can control my tongue, I'll be able to control my whole body.[91] I can't do this own my own, but I know I can do it with Your help. God, help me to think before I speak and to listen more than I talk. I want to use my words to encourage people and never to hurt people. Please fill my mouth with words that praise and glorify You. I really don't want to gossip and I really do want to please You with my words. I'm sorry for all the times I've messed up, but I know You're helping me to change. And because You are so good, I pray all those awful things I've said in the past won't be held against me.

God, when I'm with friends who are gossiping, help me to set a good example and not give in and join the gossip. You've called me to live with high standards, and I don't want to compromise in any way. Thanks for the Holy Spirit who helps me to watch what I say and shows me areas I need to change. And God, if there's anyone I've hurt with my words, I pray that You show me those people. I want to apologize and make things right. In Jesus' name, please give me strength and grace to do the right thing. You reward me when I seek You and strive to please You.[92] I'm excited about my life and all the great things You have in store for me. I know that because I've committed to speak positive and godly words, my life is good! Amen.

thoughts

For I know the thoughts that I think toward you, says the LORD, thoughts of peace and not of evil, to give you a future and a hope.

Jeremiah 29:11 NKJV

Oh my goodness, it's so awesome to think that number one, God is thinking about you and me, but even more, that His thoughts include our future. He wants us to be so blessed. Our responsibility then is to get our thoughts in line with His. Are you thinking and saying you're going to have a crummy life? If you are, *stop!* Don't waste one more second thinking negatively. Remember, you have been bought with a great price.[93] Whose daughter are you? If you want to be like Jesus, you have to think like your heavenly Father.

Have you ever heard people say, "she's got her daddy's eyes" or "she acts just like her dad?" Well, that's exactly what we're going for. I believe you're going to begin thinking like your heavenly Father;

knowing without a doubt He has an incredible future for you. The Bible says His thoughts are higher than our thoughts and His ways are higher than ours.[94] That's what we want to reach for, and we can because He is at work in us to do His will and good pleasure.[95] He wants His best for us even more than we do.

If you've been thinking wrong, it's not too late to change to God's thoughts about you. And don't let it stop there. Ask Him to give you His thoughts and heart concerning your family, friends, teachers, pastors, and all those connected with you. What a way to help and bless others!

what's a girl to do?
when she needs wisdom

Consider it pure joy, my brothers, whenever you face trials of many kinds, because you know that the testing of your faith develops perseverance. Perseverance must finish its work so that you may be mature and complete, not lacking anything. If any of you lacks wisdom, he should ask God, who gives generously to all without finding fault, and it will be given to him. But when he asks, he must believe and not doubt, because he who doubts is like a wave of the sea, blown and tossed by the wind. That man should not think he will receive anything from the Lord; he is a double-minded man, unstable in all he does.

James 1:2-8 NIV

wisdom

The fruit of the [uncompromisingly] righteous is a tree of life, and he who is wise captures human lives [for God, as a fisher of men—he gathers and receives them for eternity].

Proverbs 11:30 AMP

Father,

Thank You Your Word says if I lack wisdom I can ask You and You will give it to me generously, without finding fault.[96] So I do ask You for wisdom, believing You will give it to me. I hear Your voice, the voice of the good Shepherd and a stranger's voice I will not follow.[97] I hear Your counsel, receive Your instruction, and accept correction so I am wise in the time to come. Your Word also says whoever finds wisdom finds life and receives favor from you Lord.[98] Help me Father to be wise in all my decisions and more than anything help me to bring souls to You. You said if I capture human lives for You, I am truly wise. I ask this in Jesus' name. Amen.

God time

For I am convinced that neither death
nor life, neither angels nor demons,
neither the present nor the future, nor
any powers, neither height nor depth,
nor anything else in all creation, will
be able to separate us from the love
of God that is in Christ Jesus our Lord.

Romans 8:38-39 NIV

God is love and we can't do anything to make
Him love us anymore. So how do we get closer to
God? Well, I like to say if you move to Canada
you'll be as close as you can get to God—just
teasin'. That's because I grew up there and get a
little homesick once in awhile.

So anyway, how do we get to know the Lord
better? Well, how do we get to know our friends
better? How do we get to know our family better?
I'd have to say by spending time with them. We
need to commit to any relationship. I learn things
about my own husband and my three sons by
spending time with them. We have to set aside

time to spend together. We talk and listen to each other. If we care about our friends we make time for them.

Just the fact that you're reading this *little pink book of prayers* is a sure sign that you want to grow closer to Jesus. We need to seek God with our whole heart. His Word is a love letter to us and it is alive and full of power. As we not only read the Scriptures but plant them in our heart, they grow and we will hear from God.

Prayer is our way to talk to the Lord straight from our heart. He hears us and answers us. We have the best example of prayer in our Lord Jesus. And when we aren't sure how to pray about something, the Holy Spirit will help us. The more we spend time in God's presence, the more time we will want to spend with Him and the more certain we'll know His voice. God is so good and is always listening to our prayers. We can be sure He will answer in the way that's the very best for us and others we are praying for.

1 John 5:14,15 (AMP) says, "And this is the confidence (the assurance, the privilege of boldness)

which we have in Him: [we are sure] that if we ask anything (make any request) according to His will (in agreement with His own plan), He listens to and hears us. And if (since) we [positively] know that He listens to us in whatever we ask, we also know [with settled and absolute knowledge] that we have [granted us as our present possessions] the requests made of Him."

"The most valuable thing the Psalms do for me is to express the same delight in God which made David dance."⁹⁹

—C.S. Lewis

20th Century Novelist and Academic

trinity

God the Father knew you and chose you long ago, and his Spirit has made you holy. As a result, you have obeyed him and have been cleansed by the blood of Jesus Christ. May God give you more and more grace and peace.

1 Peter 1:2 NLT

This verse mentions all three persons or members of the Trinity (3 persons in 1)—God the Father, God the Son, and God the Holy Spirit. God, your Father, chose you long before you chose Him. God, the Son, died for you even though you were a sinner. God, the Holy Spirit, lives in you as a Christian young woman to be your helper and guide every single day. All three Persons of the Trinity had a part in your salvation and can play a vital role each day in how you live your life.

Because of the redemptive work of God the Son, God the Father sent to you the Holy Spirit to cleanse you, restore you, and renew you to complete wholeness. *All* of your sin was washed away—not just part. You need to see yourself for who you are today, not who you were before you experienced this new beginning because this is how God (the Trinity) sees you now—Pure! Holy! Cleansed! Lovely! His Daughter!

You have been called to be a child of the Living God and He has set you apart (from the world) for His purposes and plans. Be assured that if you were chosen by the Father (and you were), saved by the blood of the Son, and filled with the Holy Spirit, God (the Trinity) has specific plans and purposes just for you.

Get out there and start living and being who you truly are—a daughter of the most high God! You are so special to Him.

who I am

Father God,

Thank You for creating me in Your image.[100] *You said in the Bible that I am remarkably and wonderfully made, and I pray You help me to really believe and accept that.*[101] *Help me not to compare myself to my friends or to celebrities.*

I pray I will see myself the way You see me, and I will love myself the way You love me. When I start to feel bad about myself, I ask You to reveal to me the thoughts that are not from You. Help me to separate Your thoughts about me from lies. Show me if there are things I believe about myself that really aren't true, because I only want to believe Your truth.

God, I pray I really see the beauty in me. I don't want to be puffed up and prideful, but I also don't want to feel condemned and dejected. You said in the Bible it isn't fancy hairstyles and jewelry that make girls attractive; it's the hidden, spiritual person, and its gentleness and submission to

You.[102] Father God, give me a deeper understanding of what that really means.

God, You also said that when I look to You, I become radiant.[103] So I humble myself before You and commit to always look to You. Show me how to dress, fix my hair, and do my make-up in ways flattering to me. I know I represent You everywhere I go and I ask You to help me to be a true example of You.

God, help me to be disciplined to take care of my body. You said our bodies are Yours anyway.[104] I want to make wise choices to live a long, healthy life and do everything You've called me to do, in Jesus' name.

righteousness

Namely, the righteousness of God which comes by believing with personal trust and confident reliance on Jesus Christ (the Messiah). [And it is meant] for all who believe.

Romans 3:22 AMP

Righteousness is a big word, but it has a very simple meaning. Righteousness means free from guilt or sin.[105] When you ask Jesus Christ into your heart, your heavenly Father declares you "righteous".[106] But it also does something else for you. It empowers you to live the way He wants you to live.[107] You will always have choices to make—good ones or otherwise—but you have the power of God's goodness in you to choose righteously. All sin, big or little, cuts us off from the Lord, Who is holy. Separation happens because of sin, but every sin can be forgiven. Because of the sacrifice of Jesus, when you accept Him as Lord, your heavenly Father sees you as though you had never sinned. Is our God not awesome!

Matthew 5:6 says, "Blessed are they which do hunger and thirst after righteousness, for they shall be filled." When we become His righteousness through salvation, God puts a hunger and a thirst in our hearts for Him. We begin to want to live a "righteous" life. You will find you long to know more about Him and how to please Him in your thoughts, your actions, your friendships, and your family. By daily reading His Word and praying (simply talking to Him), your "hunger and thirst" will be satisfied.

So feed that hunger and quench that thirst for Him every day!

think pink

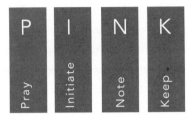

P I N K

Pray Initiate Note Keep

our heavenly Father

Oh yes, you shaped me first inside, then out; you formed me in my mother's womb. I thank you, High God—you're breathtaking! Body and soul, I am marvelously made! I worship in adoration—what a creation! You know me inside and out, You know every bone in my body; You know exactly how I was made, bit by bit, how I was sculpted from nothing into something. Like an open book, you watched me grow from conception to birth; all the stages of my life were spread out before you, The days of my life all prepared before I'd even lived one day.

Psalms 139:13-16 MSG

worship is relationship

Did you know that, as believers, we can never disappoint God? There is nothing we can do that would ever make God love us any more or any less. We can't earn God's love, and we don't have to! When He looks at us, He looks at us through the perfection of Jesus' sacrifice on the cross for us.[108] Isn't that great news?

Psalm 139 shows us He intricately planned every part of who we are. He thought through every detail of who we would be. He looked through time and knew every decision and every choice we would make. Nothing we've done takes Him by surprise. He created us even though He knew we would fail sometimes and make mistakes. Why? Because He loved us that much.[109]

You see, God is complete in every way, but He desires relationship with His creation. The first step in understanding worship, is understanding God's love.[110] And any being that gives love, desires love in return. This was God's whole purpose in creating man in the first place.

Revelation, Chapter 4 gives us a glimpse into the throne room of Heaven where 24 elders and four living creatures praise God constantly. In verse 11, the elders say, "Thou art worthy, O Lord, to receive glory and honour and power: for thou hast created all things, and for thy pleasure they are and were created." Isn't that cool? This tells us God's purpose in creation is for His pleasure. It pleased Him to create you! It ministers to God when we just stop and tell Him we love Him, and we are so thankful for the good things in our lives.

Worship is our lifeline to God. It's our connection to His very presence! It's our way of just telling Him we love Him, and His way of telling us He loves us. Before we can understand anything else about worship, we must understand God adores us and loves it when we take time to connect with Him!

worship: loving God

Dear Lord,

I Thank You I can love You because You loved me first.[111] I love You. Help me to begin to know and understand Your love for me like never before. Thank You for choosing to create me; for thinking through every little detail of my life. [112] You are amazing and wonderful and I worship You, in Jesus' name, Amen.

worship is power

We just read how God loves it when we worship, but did you know that He also designed worship to bless you? Isn't that so like God? He loves it when we give, so He can give to us even more. Here are a few benefits God gives us when we praise Him:

Strength: Nehemiah 8:10 says "the joy of the LORD is your strength." When we praise the Lord, it literally strengthens us from the inside out! Proverbs 17:22 (NLT) says, "A cheerful heart is good medicine, but a broken spirit saps a person's strength." There are numerous medical studies proving that a positive attitude strengthens our immune systems, helps us to fight disease, and causes us to live longer. Literally, the joy of the Lord is medicine to our body!

Peace: Philippians 4:6,7 (NLT) says, "Don't worry about anything; instead, pray about everything. Tell God what you need, and thank him for all he has done. Then you will experience God's peace, which exceeds anything we can understand. His peace will guard your hearts and minds as you live in Christ Jesus." When we thank God for all He has done for us, the Bible tells us that He will guard us with an overwhelming peace in both our heart and mind. 2 Timothy 1:7 (NLT) says, "For God has not given us a spirit of fear and timidity, but of power, love, and self-discipline." The *Amplified Bible* describes "self-discipline" as a "calm and well-balanced mind." Here God has just given us a cure for stress, worry, and fear, and it's called "being thankful."

You see, when we praise and thank God we stop looking at the "bigness" of our problem, and start looking at the bigness of our God! The enemy would love nothing more than to keep our focus on the problem. Looking at the problem keeps us in self-pity and pride. Praise and thanks-giving forces us to get our attention off of the problem and onto God! It fixes our eyes on what God has done for us through the death and resurrection of Jesus!

Philippians 4:8 (NLT) tells us how we can change our focus, "Fix your thoughts on what is true, and honorable, and right, and pure, and lovely, and admirable. Think about things that are excellent and worthy of praise." When we worship God with a thankful heart, we are strengthening our faith in Him. When our faith is strong we can't help but praise Him. And when we have a thankful heart that praises Him, we are full of joy and peace. I don't think it gets much better than that!

power to win

Dear Lord,

Thank You for Your joy which is my strength![113] Thank You for helping me to think on good things instead of on what's negative. I praise You because You are bigger than anything I could face, and You hold the answer to my every need. I worship You because You are truly an awesome God. Thank you for the power to win in every situation, in Jesus' name. I love You, Lord! Amen.

worship is a weapon

Did you know when you worship God, you defeat Satan? We see from Ezekiel 28:14-19 and Isaiah 14:13-14 Satan was an archangel in heaven named Lucifer. The Scriptures describe him as a beautiful being, and many scholars believe that he may have been the praise and worship leader of heaven. But he became jealous of the worship that belonged to God. He coveted it for himself, and he was ultimately cast out of heaven because of his pride and jealousy.

Satan is still full of jealousy toward God, and his whole plan is to stop us from praising God and to get our attention on our problems. I believe the main reason a person feels far away from God is because in their heart they've made problems bigger than God Himself. But, when we praise our Father with thankful hearts, and when our hearts and minds are fixed on Him and His Word, then we are destroying Satan's plans!

Psalm 8:2 (NLT) says, "You have taught children and infants to tell of your strength, silencing your enemies and all who oppose you." On Palm Sunday, when Jesus enters into Jerusalem, He quotes from Psalm 8, only he changes "to tell of your strength" to "to give you praise." I believe Jesus is revealing to us here that praise is strength (Neh. 8:10), and it's a strength that silences the enemy!

In 2 Chronicles 20, King Jehoshaphat is about to lead his army into battle. God instructs him to put the singers out front to lead the army. As they went into battle praising and worshipping God, singing, "Give thanks to the Lord; His faithful love endures forever!" (20:21), the Lord sent an ambush against the enemy armies and they were defeated.

James 4:7 (NLT) says, "So humble yourselves before God. Resist the devil, and he will flee from you." We humble ourselves before God by praising and thanking Him. True humility is recognizing it's not what we've done that brings blessing into our lives, but only through the power of Jesus. So, as we worship our God, Satan takes off running because he can't stand to stay in a place that's full of the love of God!

defeating the enemy

Dear Lord,

*Thank You that as I praise You, Satan has to go![114]
Thank you that as I worship You, You fill me up
with Your strength and power. Thank You for
being so good, and for loving me unconditionally.
You are truly an awesome God! Even if my circumstances look bad, I praise You because I know You
will work all things together for good in my life.[115]
I cannot be defeated, in Jesus' name, Amen.*

the trouble tree

I hired a plumber to help me restore an old farm-house and after he had just finished a rough first day on the job, a flat tire made him lose an hour of work, his electric drill quit, and his ancient one-ton truck refused to start. While I drove him home, he sat in stony silence.

On arriving, he invited me in to meet his family. As we walked towards the front door, he paused briefly at a small tree, touching the tips of the branches with both hands. When opening the door he underwent an amazing transformation. His face was wreathed in smiles and he hugged his two small children and gave his wife a kiss.

Afterward he walked me to the car. We passed the tree and my curiosity got the better of me. I asked him about what I had seen him do earlier.

"Oh, that's my trouble tree," he replied. "I know I can't help having troubles on the job, but one thing's for sure, those troubles don't belong in the house with my wife and the children, so I just hang them up on the tree every night when I come home and ask God to take care of them. Then in the morning I pick them up again."

"Funny thing is," he smiled, "when I come out in the morning to pick 'em up, there aren't nearly as many as I remember hanging up the night before."

Anonymous

carrots, eggs, & coffee

A carrot, an egg, and a cup of coffee—you will never look at a cup of coffee the same way again.

A young woman went to her mother and told her about her life and how things were so hard for her. She did not know how she was going to make it and wanted to give up, she was tired of fighting and struggling. It seemed as one problem was solved, a new one arose.

Her mother took her to the kitchen. She filled three pots with water and placed each on a high fire. Soon the pots came to boil. In the first she placed carrots, in the second she placed eggs, and in the last she placed ground coffee beans. She let them sit and boil without saying a word.

In about twenty minutes she turned off the burners. She fished the carrots out and placed them in a bowl. She pulled the eggs out and placed them in a bowl. Then she ladled the coffee out and placed it in a bowl. Turning to her daughter, she asked, "Tell me what you see."

"Carrots, eggs, and coffee," she replied.

Her mother brought her closer and asked her to feel the carrots. She did and noted that they were soft. The mother then asked the daughter to take an egg and break it. After pulling off the shell, she observed the hard boiled egg. Finally, the mother asked the daughter to sip the coffee. The daughter smiled as she tasted its rich aroma. The daughter then asked, "What does it mean, Mother?"

Her mother explained that each of these objects had faced the same adversity: boiling water. Each reacted differently. The carrot went in strong, hard, and unrelenting. However, after being subjected to the boiling water, it softened and became weak. The egg had been fragile. Its thin outer shell had protected its liquid interior, but after sitting through the boiling water, its inside became hardened. The ground coffee beans were unique, however. After they were in the boiling water, they had changed the water.

"Which are you?" she asked her daughter. "When adversity knocks on

your door, how do you respond? Are you
a carrot, an egg or a coffee bean?"

Author Unknown

Think of this: Which am I? Am I the carrot that
seems strong, but with pain and adversity do I
wilt, become soft, and lose my strength?

Am I the egg that starts with a malleable heart,
but changes with the heat? Did I have a fluid
spirit, but after a death, a breakup, a financial
hardship or some other trial, have I become hardened and stiff? Does my shell look the same, but
on the inside am I bitter and tough with a stiff
spirit and hardened heart?

Or am I like the coffee bean? The bean actually
changes the hot water, the very circumstance that
brings the pain. When the water gets hot, it
releases the fragrance and flavor. If you are like
the bean, when things are at their worst, you get
better and change the situation around you.
When the hour is the darkest and trials are their
greatest do you elevate yourself to another level?
How do you handle adversity? Are you a carrot,
an egg, or a coffee bean?

May you have enough happiness to make you sweet, enough trials to make you strong, enough sorrow to keep you human, and enough hope to make you happy.

The happiest of people don't necessarily have the best of everything; they just make the most of everything that comes along their way. The brightest future will always be based on a forgotten past; you can't go forward in life until you let go of your past failures and heartaches.

When you were born, you were crying and everyone around you was smiling. Live your life so at the end, you're the one who is smiling and everyone around you is crying.

May we all be *coffee!*

think pink

P — Pray

I — Initiate

N — Note

K — Keep

PSALM 5:2-3 AMP

Hear the sound of my cry, my King
and my God, for to You do I pray.
In the morning You hear my voice,
O Lord; in the morning I prepare
[a prayer, a sacrifice]
for You and watch and wait
[for You to speak to my heart].

waiting…hoping…expecting—
let's do it!

My family has a dog named Muffy. She is a soft coated Wheaten Terrier that looks a little bit like a cross between a small sheep dog and a real fluffy stuffed animal, along the line of a bear. One of the things we just love about her is how much she loves people. She doesn't know a stranger. Shortly after we got her we read that Wheatens are known for a little custom they do called the Wheaten greetin'. The minute anyone comes through the front door they automatically receive the greetin'.

Let me tell you…this is a dream dog for any person who needs affirmation in their life. I get such a kick out of her because she's really got it down when it comes to *waiting* and *hoping* and *expecting*. She is such an optimist.

When my husband, Blaine, drives up on the driveway or any of my three boys come to see us, she goes berserk—running to the window, then the door, back and forth again and again until that door opens.

Then the greeting begins. She jumps and jumps, wags that tail, and kisses and twirls then does it all over again. If Blaine has to go back out to the truck to get something else…yep, it's like he's been gone for a week. It happens all over again.

Well one day I was just thinking about what it means to wait and expect and hope on the Lord and it struck me that Muffy was a good little example of how we should come into God's presence—always so hopeful and with great expectation, knowing that God is going to receive our affection and we can't wait to hear what He has to say to us. You know He loves to even sing over us and embraces us. He never tires of showing us His favor. There is a time of waiting but we are waiting for a faithful Father Who will never leave us hopeless.

So girls when we go to God in prayer, remember as we wait on Him, expect to hear His voice. He wants to tell us incredible things about our lives and even give us wisdom to help others. Don't forget that without a doubt, He is listening to you—just waiting to hear from a thankful daughter and answer the cries of her heart.

closing thoughts

I am convinced that if you know that you know
how much God loves you, nothing can stop you
from running the race that He has called you to
and becoming the woman of God that He
created you to be. We are all a work in progress
and along the way, no matter what obstacles we
come up against, we can have the assurance of
knowing that God's love for us is:

- eternal
- unending
- everlasting
- relentless
- abiding
- constant
- unchanging
- steadfast
- forgiving
- and oh, so full of grace

Always remember these things. Never give up.
Make a decision to forever put your faith and trust
and hope in Jesus. Be that girl—the one who

makes choices based on God's Word and a prayerful heart.

When you mess up, be that girl who runs to the Lord, asks forgiveness, knows that He never left you, and will continue speak to you and hear your prayer. "The LORD is close to all who call on him, yes, to all who call on him in truth. He grants the desires of those who fear him; he hears their cries for help and rescues them" (Ps. 145:18-19 NLT).

Our relationship with our heavenly Father will only become stronger as we direct our passion and love, our time and our voice, towards Him. What a future God has for us. I don't mind tellin' ya', I'm 48 and more excited than ever to hear from the Lord as to what's ahead. What incredible things does He have in store for my husband and my three sons? How is He directing all of the amazing people in our church and others in our lives? I want to be a part of that by hearing God's voice in how I can encourage and cheer them on. Wow. Can you say that backwards...wow! (I always tell my boys that "Mom" is "wow" upside down.)

Anyway, what spectacular adventures are in store for you? "This is God's Message, the God who made earth, made it livable and lasting, known everywhere as God: 'Call to me and I will answer you. I'll tell you marvelous and wondrous things that you could never figure out on your own'" (Jer. 33:2-3 MSG).

Please live life everyday knowing how much you are loved by God and listen to those desires He so gently places in your heart. Be the young woman who knows she is not too young to pray and hear from God. As we surrender our lives and commit to spend time in God's Word, prayer, and worship (in His presence) our lives and everyone around us will forever be transformed. Just one touch from the King changes everything.

As I've been writing to you in this little book, I have fallen more in love with Jesus than ever. *Thank you* for letting me into *your* life. I've been so refreshed and challenged to be a better wife, mom, sister, aunt, daughter, and friend. My prayer is that more than anything, we are all more devoted to wholeheartedly follow Jesus in our call to prayer. As God's daughters we will say, "Lord teach us to pray!" And He will.

Grace and peace be multiplied to you my little sister.

Love,
Cathy

think pink

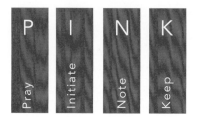

P S A L M   3 2 : 8   N I R V

I will guide you and teach you the way you should go. I will give you good advice and watch over you.

pink
prayer

prayer of salvation

God loves you—no matter who you are, no matter what your past. God loves you so much that He gave His one and only begotten Son for you. The Bible tells us that "whoever believes in him shall not perish but have eternal life" (John 3:16 NIV). Jesus laid down His life and rose again so that we could spend eternity with Him in heaven and experience His absolute best on earth. If you would like to receive Jesus into your life, say the following prayer out loud and mean it from your heart.

Heavenly Father, I come to You admitting that I am a sinner. Right now, I choose to turn away from sin, and I ask You to cleanse me of all unrighteousness. I believe that Your Son, Jesus, died on the cross to take away my sins. I also believe that He rose again from the dead so that I might be forgiven of my sins and made righteous through faith in Him. I call upon the name of Jesus Christ to be the Savior and Lord of my life. Jesus, I choose to follow You and ask that You fill me with the power of the Holy Spirit. I declare that right now I am a child of God. I am free from sin and full of the righteousness of God. I am saved in Jesus' name. Amen.

If you prayed this prayer to receive Jesus Christ as your Savior for the first time, please contact us on the Web at **www.harrisonhouse.com** to receive a free book. Or you may write to us at:

Harrison House

P.O. Box 35035

Tulsa, Oklahoma 74153

endnotes

1   Author unknown

2   Ephesians 2:10

3   1 Corinthians 6:19-20

4   Revelation 3:11

5   Philippians 2:12-15

6   Darlene Zschech, *Extravagant Worship: Holy, Holy, Holy is the Lord God Almighty Who Was, and Is, and Is to Come* (Bethany House, 2004).

7   John 16:24

8   Matthew 5:14

9   Proverbs 28:1

10 2 Timothy 1:7

11 Luke 18:27

12 Joshua 1:7

13 1 John 4:18

14 2 Timothy 1:7

15 Philippians 4:7

16 Philippians 4:9

17 http://www.thoughts-about-god.com/quotes/quotes-prayer.htm

18 Hebrews 13:5

[19] See Psalm 23:3, Proverbs 6:22, Isaiah 58:11 and John 16:13.

[20] James 1:17

[21] John 10:10

[22] Psalm 32:8

[23] Psalm 119:105

[24] Deuteronomy 31:8

[25] Ephesians 2:10

[26] See John 10:1-14.

[27] See Acts 1-3.

[28] John 14:17

[29] See Matthew 26:28 and Luke 6:37.

[30] http://www.articlealley.com/article_209961_27.html

[31] 2 Corinthians 5:7

[32] John 14:17

[33] Acts 13:38

[34] Isaiah 1:18

[35] Mark 11:25

[36] Philippians 2:13

[37] http://www.merriam-webster.com/dictionary, s.v. "beset."

[38] See Exodus 2 and 2 Samuel 11-12.

[39] Proverbs 29:18

40   Jeremiah 29:11

41   1 Samuel 13:14

42   http://thinkexist.com/quotes/alex_haley/

43   Proverbs 3:5–6 NIV

44   Proverbs 19:22 AMP

45   Romans 8:11

46   Isaiah 53:4-5

47   Psalm 107:19-20

48   Romans 5:17

49   Proverbs 4:23

50   James 1:5

51   Psalm 33:18

52   Philippians 3:14

53   Romans 5:13

54   http://www.brainyquote.com/quotes/quotes/b/billy-graha385020.html

55   Psalm 139:12-16

56   1 Peter 3:4

57   http://www.merriam-webster.com/dictionary,   s.v. "hospital."

58   Ephesians 6:2

59   Proverbs 22:6

60   Romans 5:5

61 2 Peter 1:2

62 http://www.petsinpastel.com/quotes.htm

63 George Eliot, 'Mr. Gilfil's Love Story,' Scenes of Clerical Life, 1857 English novelist (1819 - 1880)

64 http://www.gaylasgarden.com/pets/bed.htm

65 James 4:7

66 Isaiah 54:17

67 Ephesians 6:13-17

68 Ephesians 6:18

69 1 Corinthians 1:30

70 Matthew 18:18

71 1 Peter 2:24

72 Deuteronomy 30:9, Philippians 4:19

73 Proverbs 18:10

74 Psalm 34:7

75 Matthew 21:22

76 Matthew 9:37

77 Dictionary.com. Dictionary.com Unabridged (v 1.1). Random House, Inc. http://dictionary.reference.com/browse/serve, s.v. "serve."

78 Nehemiah 8:10, I Peter 4:11

79 Matthew 20:28

80 Deuteronomy 31:6

81 Acts 1:8

82 Acts 2:4

83 Romans 8:26

84 Isaiah 61:3

85 See Galatians 5:22, Matthew 5:16.

86 Jeremiah 29:11

87 Isaiah 40:28-31

88 Deuteronomy 31:6

89 2 Timothy 1:6

90 Deuteronomy 31:6

91 James 3:2

92 Hebrews 11:6

93 1 Corinthians 6:20

94 Isaiah 55:8-9

95 Philippians 2:13

96 James 1:5

97 John 10:4-5

98 Proverbs 8:35

99 http://www.comnett.net/~rex/cslewis.htm

100 Genesis 1:27

101 Psalm 139:14

102 1 Peter 3:3-4

103 Psalm 34:5

[104] 1 Corinthians 6:19

[105] http://www.merriam-webster.com/dictionary, s.v. "righteous."

[106] Romans 5:17

[107] Hebrews 10:15-17

[108] Romans 5:17

[109] John 3:16

[110] 1 John 4:8

[111] 1 John 4:19

[112] Psalm 139:13-16

[113] Nehemiah 8:10

[114] James 4:7

[115] Romans 8:28

For more than a quarter of a century, Cathy Bartel has served alongside her husband, Blaine, in what they believe is the hope of the world, the local church. For the better part of two decades, they served their pastor, Willie George, in building one of America's most respected churches, Church on the Move, in Tulsa, Oklahoma. Blaine and Cathy helped found Oneighty, which has become one of the most emulated youth ministries in the past 15 years, reaching 2,500–3,000 students weekly under their leadership.

While Blaine is known for his communication and leadership skills, Cathy is known for her heart and hospitality. Blaine is quick to recognize her "behind the scenes" gifting to lift and encourage people as one of the great strengths of their ministry together. Her effervescent spirit and contagious smile open the door for her ministry each day, whether she's in the church or at the grocery store.

Cathy is currently helping Blaine raise a new community of believers committed to relevant ministry and evangelism as pastors of Northstar Church in the growing north Dallas suburb of Frisco, Texas.

Cathy's greatest reward has come in the raising of her 3 boys—Jeremy, Dillon, and Brock. Today, each son is serving Christ with his unique abilities and is deeply involved in Blaine and Cathy's ongoing ministry.

To contact Cathy Bartel please write to:

Cathy Bartel
Serving America's Future
P.O. Box 691923
Tulsa, Oklahoma 74169
www.blainebartel.com

*Please include your prayer requests
and comments when you write.*

pink is for princess...

...and being a princess can be a challenge. discover your heavenly Father's hotline for all the answers in friendships, school, family, and life. find the grace to become something great!

every teen girl's little pink book special gift edition includes three complete works in one volume: **little pink book, little pink book for girlfriends,** and **little pink book on gab.**

ISBN: 978-1-57794-909-1